# PRAISE FOR *PLAN OF ACTION*

"So many of us are dissatisfied with our lives. We need to change, but how? Randy Linville shows you how. He has led businesses at the highest level and has a storehouse of wisdom to share. *Plan of Action* distills the key principles that made Linville successful. My advice is to get this book and follow its advice!"

**—Seth Barnes, founder, Adventures in Missions and World Race**

"Randy's text is what I sometimes call Kool-Aid without water: valuable information richly condensed. My highest compliment is that I'll give copies to my three sons, each of whom can 'water' the guidance from his own life experience and be richly blessed for it."

**—Jay Bennett, chairman of the board, National Christian Foundation**

"Randy offers some very practical and wise guidance as you navigate daily life in the marketplace. It is great to see someone with his experiences be able to communicate such important lessons that all of us need to hear in a very clear and concise way."

**—Rod Brenneman, former CEO Butterball and Seaboard Foods**

"Everyone who knew Bob knew he had no idea he'd have a legacy. He just thought he did what he was called to do for his time. He'd be pleased to know that his work with leaders lives on in their influence and in new generations."

**—Linda Buford, wife of Bob Buford, founder of The Halftime Institute**

"Randy has lived an extraordinary life, gained valuable wisdom, and now shares his life lessons with clarity and brevity. Having had the pleasure of working with Randy, I know him to be a man of immense competence, character, and meaningful contributions. Enjoy your journey."

**—Joe Calhoon, author of *Prioritize!, On the Same Page, and The One Hour Plan for Growth***

"Randy's generosity and humor in sharing pivotal moments during his transition will ease this fragile and important stage of life for many. The cadence of his storytelling and easy dialogue bring the reader along, offering that much-needed pause to consider what brings joy, satisfaction, and fulfillment in a next phase of life. Transitions are hard, and this book helps with practical insight and humor."

**—Debbie Dellinger, director of external engagement, My Next Season**

"Like reading a modern-day Book of Proverbs, Randy Linville's *Plan of Action* is filled with wisdom gained through lived experience. It is an inspiring, practical, and helpful guide to living the good life."

**—Adam Hamilton, senior pastor, The United Methodist Church of the Resurrection; best-selling author of *The Walk***

"*Plan of Action* could well be titled *A Life Well Lived: A Timeless Manuscript for Living a Successful, Fulfilling, and Rich Life That Glorifies God!* This book is a trove of practical, proven, and time-tested principles guaranteed to ignite new levels of vision, passion, conviction, and action in your life."

**—Drew Hiss, founder and CEO, Acumen**

"Every farmer understands the value of good soil and nutrients as the foundation for a great crop, and without those, nothing will grow. Randy has been a farmer and CEO and involved in numerous nonprofit and industry organizations. His experiences and thoughts highlighted in this book can help us reflect on ourselves and the soil into which we are sewing. With planning and effort, we can improve our crops, whether that be in our personal, family, spiritual, or professional lives by following the steps of action Randy has laid out in this book."

**—Kent Horsager, CEO, Compass Strategic Investments**

"So many great tools. So many great stories."

**—Dr. Rhonda Kehlbeck, vice president of admissions, The Halftime Institute**

"Randy's wisdom and practical advice are a guide to living a life of purpose. *Plan of Action* is filled with nuggets that will help you navigate life especially in times of change."

**—Mark Linsz, cofounder and managing partner, My Next Season**

"I have known Randy Linville for decades. Randy is a highly respected business leader and an incredibly disciplined person who is grounded in his Midwestern agricultural roots. Randy's natural instincts are to find effective processes to help simplify the complex, to clarify and align the goals, and ultimately to improve the outcomes. All of that shines through in his book, *Plan of Action*. I recommend reading the book with pen in hand to learn from this proven leader."

**—Todd McQueen, board member, The Scoular Company**

"Randy has written an incredible 'Checklist for Life' that is truly a personal development guide for everyone seeking their North Star and accepting the challenges of rebalancing their lives with reliance on faith, family, and fellowship. Our shared experiences of growing up on a farm with Christian parents in a task-oriented life taught us the value of hard work and making decisions that developed our leadership skills at an early age. The hardships experienced in farming prepared us for challenges in our food and agriculture careers, and for these experiences we are forever grateful. Our mutual experiences with FarmHouse Fraternity and its mission as a 'builder of men' with a faith-based purpose no doubt shaped our lives to become servant leaders in our personal lives and professional careers. Randy's application of Scripture to our daily routines are time tested and fundamental to the checklists he has shared with his readers. I am thankful for Randy's humble and candid sharing of personal and thoughtful insights on how to organize our daily lives and plan for the future."

**—Jeff Muchow, managing partner, Bio-Clean Solutions LLC**

"In a time when we are inundated with more information than we ever imagined possible, it is refreshing to encounter rare nuggets of timeless wisdom we so desperately need. As a faithful follower of Jesus and a seasoned business leader, Randy Linville has patiently discovered and generously shared bite-size pieces of practical guidance for the challenges and complexities of daily life in the modern marketplace. *Plan of Action* will inspire and enrich your life and work."

**—Tom Nelson, pastor, Christ Community Church and president, Made To Flourish**

"Randy Linville is a walking billboard of The Halftime Institute message, another legacy to Bob Buford's influential life. You can't read *Plan of Action* without being better for it."

**—Dean Niewolney, CEO, The Halftime Institute**

"This book is a practical collection of lessons and ideas that are not theory but are so important for us all to practice. Randy's personal stories enhance the lessons he has to teach."

**—Kevin Rauckman, executive director, KC Fellows;**
**retired CFO and treasurer, Garmin Ltd.**

"We all need a plan of action today to help guide us to tomorrow. Few writers bring this level of insight and collected wisdom."

**—Clayton Smith, pastor, speaker, and author of**
***At the Crossroads: Leadership Lessons for the Second Half of Life***

"*Plan of Action* is an incredible collection of life insights from someone who has led well—from the highest levels of corporate America to the church and other service organizations. Read this book once, and you'll find challenge, encouragement, and redirection. Then come back to it over and over for one-chapter-at-a-time reminders of why you found it so useful in the first place. Every role on the team (leader, supporter, teammate) in every arena (business, church, not-for-profit, school, family) will benefit from *Plan of Action*."

**—Brent Vander Ark, vice president of financial service, Kansas City Southern Railway**

"Randy draws on over four decades of leadership experience in both the for-profit and nonprofit sectors in this very practical guide to living and leading well. He weaves together his and other leaders' experiences, biblical principles, and reflections, culminating in practical suggestions to get you thinking about how you, too, can skillfully develop a plan of action for life."

—**Dr. Stan W. Wallace, CEO, Global Scholars and host of the *College Faith* podcast**

"I read *Plan of Action* thinking how a business student or classroom full of business students would gain from this book."

—**Shari Wilkins, program director of adult Sunday school and group connections,**
**The United Methodist Church of the Resurrection**

"*Plan of Action* is a best practice manual for living a life of wisdom and significance. Randy's blend of the practical and spiritual is inviting and inspirational. I love the generational aspect of paying forward Randy's life lessons to help the next generation run well. The Toolbox at the end is a rich resource for life and godliness. I look forward to using the book in our disciple-making networks in Kansas City."

—**David Wooddell, The Navigators, Kansas City**

# PLAN
## *of*
# ACTION

### NAVIGATING A LIFE OF
### CHANGE, WORK, AND FAITH

# RANDY LINVILLE
## WITH NANCY LOVELL

Publisher's Cataloging-in-Publication data

Names: Linville, Randy, author. | Lovell, Nancy, author.
Title: Plan of action : navigating a life of change, work, and faith / by Randy Linville ; with Nancy Lovell.
Description: Includes bibliographical references. | Nashville, TN: Clearsight Publishing, 2021.
Identifiers: ISBN 9781736158104 (hardcover) | 9781736158111 (ebook)
Subjects: LCSH Business planning. | Strategic planning. | Business—Religious aspects—Christianity. | Work—Religious aspects—Christianity. | Christian living. | BISAC RELIGION / Christian Living / Personal Growth | BUSINESS & ECONOMICS / Personal Success | SELF-HELP / Personal Growth / Success
Classification: LCC HF5388 .L56 2021 | DDC 658.4/012–dc23

Printed in the United States of America
First printing May 2021

*For my parents, whose wisdom and love*
*continue to give me life.*

*"Plans are useless. Planning is everything."*

—General Dwight D. Eisenhower

# CONTENTS

# FOREWORD

Twenty years ago, when I met Randy Linville, I was a fresh-faced college graduate, just starting with The FarmHouse Foundation. Randy was a FarmHouse Fraternity alumnus and a generous and inventive donor. Two years later, he'd begin a six-year tenure on our board of trustees: four of them on our executive committee, two as chair.

In 2007, Randy was chair when my boss, Bob Off, retired as executive director. Having just spearheaded a new strategic plan, Randy and the board began a nationwide search to replace Bob, looking at alumni across the fraternity and fundraising professionals in other nonprofits. I was the sole internal candidate, a female and a nonmember. Could I become the first (and still only) female CEO of a men's fraternity foundation?

In the end, happily, the answer was yes. My skills, talent, and potential won the day, Randy told me. But it was still a leap of faith. I was twenty-seven years old and about to have my first baby. Randy, the trustees, our staff, and alumni all stepped up, and our educational foundation grew.

Now Randy became my mentor, confidant, and guide. Both of us lived in Kansas City, allowing us to review strategies and issues at monthly lunches. I'd bring questions; he'd bring his undivided attention, sound advice, and business mind. He'd pick up the tab, and, through the years, I picked up the equivalent of a master's degree in executive leadership.

In short, I got the gold you get in this book: a way of knowing how the world works and how to thrive in it. Like his father, Randy leads for the flourishing of those around him.

The four sections in this book—Reboot, Resolve, Respond, and Recharge—invite you to grow through counsel that may surprise you. You're urged, for instance, to both plan and to pray, and to stay ready, which involves writing. You'll see what I mean. For now, let me highlight a few practical applications of that counsel for FarmHouse.

To set it up, more than a few national fraternities are in decline. For most of them, 2 or 3 percent charitable giving by alumni is high. Yet our foundation draws double-digit alumni giving. Our graduates are in the virtuous cycle, as Randy puts it, of helping others benefit from how FarmHouse helped them. Under Randy's guidance, we dreamed and set up systems to do the following.

- **REBOOT:** We modernize our chapter houses and continually refine leadership training.

- **RESOLVE:** To advance our chapters and alumni engagement, we set plans and work them.

- **RESPONSE:** The response shows in our high alumni support and graduates poised to become tomorrow's leaders.

- **RECHARGE:** We regularly host and fund  programs like the FarmHouse Leadership Institute, a pause to help incoming officers succeed in the coming year, and the Power of 7 Seminar, a pause to mentor and, intergenerationally, share lessons learned.

At our national convention, we unleash the power of gratitude and fortify the FarmHouse culture, continually engaging students and alumni to both teach and learn from each other.

A good mentor helps us have dreams and achieve them, but not at all costs. A good mentor helps us succeed in what matters most. Life harmony, Randy calls it. Under that banner, through years of lunches, at various points in my life, Randy has been my master (see chapter 12), mentor, and friend. All three, and I'm grateful.

So who will benefit from *Plan of Action*? Almost anyone. My daughters will; I know that. The young men in our chapters will, most certainly. My peers will, and my parents will. You will because Randy deals in insights, learned and collected, to apply and live by, the kind we'd bottle if we could, and *Plan of Action* does.

I believe you'll keep this wisdom within reach—the best of a life to read for many reasons. I'm glad for your chance to know Randy too.

**Allison Rickels, CFRE**
*executive director and CEO,*
*The FarmHouse Foundation*

# INTRODUCTION

I thought I'd come to the desert to relax.

Most of my adult life I'd assumed when my career ended I'd have a next move lined up and ease into it. A project, maybe. Some philanthropy. Now at a family getaway in Arizona, I sat next to the hotel pool with a decided lack of ease. Like a punch in the gut, someday had come and I had no move.

For the last ten years I'd headed a global corporation in supply chain ag. The industry is not the point. Neither are the position or my age. The point is the restlessness rising in me for several years now, and the unmarked road it had me on.

For the last five years my sense of vocation—of doing what I was made to do—had grown stale. My company had consolidated, modernized, and staged a behemoth turnaround, and I was bored. For variety, I'd helped steer a national grain trade council into commodity markets, and I learned two things: One, it felt good to serve beyond a single company. Two, given the small staff, I loved seeing diverse volunteers serve a common good.

But inside my discontent smoldered.

That day at the hotel pool, I had with me a book about the relentless pursuit of who we're made to be. Questions in it grew fingers and poked me in the chest. *Did God create you to be a corporate exec and that's it? Is this all you'll ever do?*

Okay, okay, I thought. There's more . . . but what?

In my organized mind, my life rolled out in three sections: the first twenty-five years to grow up and learn a vocation, the next thirty to harmonize my family and career, and then . . . and then what? What was this?

These feelings had come to me twice before: when I was seventeen years old and facing high school graduation, and in midlife, when my father died. Each time, I faced change with no sense of direction. Each time, my getting to new purpose had come with hard choices and risk. *Do I leave this job? I haven't been unhappy exactly. If we move and start over, will it be worth it?*

A gut sense may or may not be a cue to change careers and move to a new city, but it's not nothing. Something needs to change. At the very least, the discontent is a dashboard signal to know more about ourselves and about God.

From my chair next to the pool, I stared at the deep end and mentally dove. I would assess my life, myself, and my options. What I wouldn't do was sleepwalk into the next section of my life. At age fifty-five, piecing together the "Who will I be?" puzzle, as it had been at ages seventeen and thirty-seven, would be labor intensive and doable.

It was time to reboot.

## GETTING TO A PLAN

I'm no expert, but I know life harmony—when our work and values sing in unison—is no accident. It may not follow a plan, but it starts with one.

The book you're holding, or reading on a screen, is not a step-by-step plan. It won't give you purpose or meaning. It won't create your identity for you. What it can do is get you there from here.

I know because every chapter has been field-tested by me and, more important, by better people than me. Achievement abhors a vacuum; every good life owes everything to other lives.

Before I was ten years old, other people were teaching me to break a challenge or project into steps and see them through. As I grew, so did the projects and the steps. In my thirties, I woke up to the almost magical power of groups, and the possibilities kept growing.

As the head of a global company, I learned to lead not by gut instinct only but by priorities and plans. Priorities require values, and values, for a Christian, point to God. As for plans, as I learned to work mine and see God work his—different from mine, often enough— my work evolved from labor to pleasure. It became a calling, the difference between work for its own sake, which can be grueling, and work in God's will, which sings out with purpose. (A leading byproduct of work in a calling is gratitude, a vastly untapped energy source. We'll talk about that later.)

Purpose is everything. Without it, nothing feels right. When we have it and lose it, we may overpay to get it back, like the military vets who re-up in spite of their poor health or having to leave their families again. Loss of purpose is why the elderly will wave goodbye to grown grandkids and sink into empty days.

When my career ended, I could have sunk or grasped for any work to stuff the hole. Thank God I somehow knew to go in search of new purpose. I fell into a group called Halftime, where people in transition help each other figure out what to do next. Insights I gained there show up throughout my story.

This book is a compass on a road to purpose and, closely linked to purpose, to dreams that come true. If you're at the end of something and unsure what to do next, this book is for you. If someone you care about has no clear direction, if he or she won't read this book and you do, it will help you listen.

All the elements for life harmony are here. Your job is to read and innovate, to adapt the ideas here into your life, your way.

## HOW TO READ *PLAN OF ACTION*

A wise man named Mortimer Adler wrote the classic *How to Read a Book*, which only sounds obvious. An active learner, Adler says, reads with pen in hand to underline, circle, number, and note: first to better retain the words on the page, and second, because no author knows everything, and our notes help us question and challenge. (You might underline that.)

In that spirit, as you begin *Plan of Action*, keep in mind these things.

1. **Read in any sequence.** The chapters stand together and alone. Chapters 1 through 3 lay a foundation; the middle chapters offer practical guidance; the final chapters cover intangibles that will, I hope, surprise you.

2. **Involve other people.** Reading with a team or a friend is likely to spark conversations, open minds, and boost your recall.

3. **Aim not to imitate but innovate.** The great adventure is not to mimic but to mix it up. When a line or a thought in *Plan of Action* stands out, underline it (see above), and consider how it applies to you.

4. **Look for direction, not conclusions.** What I call a "virtuous circle" (the opposite of a vicious one) loops from dreams to gratitude and back to new dreams. Keep *Plan of Action* at the front of your bookshelf. As you need a new dream, plan, or direction—or sense of hope—pull out the book and flip to a relevant chapter.

5. **Use the sidebars, appendices, and end-of-chapter questions.** The sidebars expand on points in the chapter. The quotes in the chapters and appendix speak for themselves. At the end of every chapter, the questions help us think.

Never underestimate the power of purpose, relationships, and the Holy Spirit. You can know yourself. You can discern your next steps. Your plan will still require faith, but far less blind guessing. God willing, what you learn will in turn affect people whose lives can affect even thousands more. That's my prayer.

Amen.

# REBOOT

**CHAPTER ONE**

# DREAM AGAIN

*An End to Smoldering Discontent*

"There are some people who live in a dream world, and there are some who face reality; and then there are those who turn one into the other."

**— Douglas H. Everett**

I n 1972 in Holcomb, Kansas, population maybe a thousand, I was in the graduating class of thirty-five students. I loved football in general, the Chiefs and Bears in particular, and Gale Sayers, "The Kansas Comet," with a boy's passion.

Sayers's autobiography, *I Am Third*, was made into a movie called *Brian's Song*, about the death of his teammate Brian Piccolo, and I saw it several times. Like a wide swath of young Americans, the book had become my bible.

At school, boys ahead of me were in the draft and getting sent to Vietnam. My lottery number was 188, low enough for soul-searching. And I came from generations of war service. Nightly newscasts served up fatality numbers and body bags. Closer to home, cancer had taken my young classmate Kathy Baier, and the school bus still drove by her stop. My uncle Glen, a test pilot, died in a plane crash, breaking our hearts. Around that time, Mrs. Rome, a farm over, died after a long and painful illness. Her five kids, close in age to the kids in my family, often came to my mom for haircuts and attention. My good friend Fred Wishon died in high school of brain cancer.

Rural Kansas offered no safeguard from tragedy, and for a seventeen-year-old boy too aware of loss and fearing change, amid rising and unnamed fears, Gale Sayers was solace on a bedroom wall. "God is first. Others are second. I am third," the poster read. The words repeated on a pendant I kept in my drawer.

Faith in God? It was decades away. For now, at holidays, weddings, and funerals, the most I could gin up was some version of the cultural religion around me. True belief would come when my father died and life without him would take more than a poster.

# GETTING TO DREAMS

It's comforting now to tell you that four decades after I left home, this time at the end of a twenty-five-year career, what came to my mind was the Gale Sayers quote.

While filling out a questionnaire about my sense of purpose, I saw myself write, "God is first. Others are second." This time the words were more than a slogan. First, they meant real faith, no cultural substitutes; second, I wanted to be a godly family man and neighbor; third, they had to do with being a leader wise in God's eyes.

"Real faith" referred also to all the years I'd lived on the fence. "Godly family man and neighbor" was a nod to my father, to his easy goodness. "Leader wise in God's eyes" was my rejection of people wise in their own eyes. No more contracts and cheap cynicism. I needed to get back to my picture of the code of the American pioneer, ground into me in West Kansas, that a person's word is a bond.

I needed my own dreams again.

The questionnaire was in a program I mentioned in the introduction: The Halftime Institute, founded and for years headed by a man named Bob Buford. Every generation has its world changers; Bob was the big one in mine. After expanding his own highly successful company, sometime in his forties he scanned the parade of commas in his net worth and shrugged. What he craved, he said, was not more success. He needed significance. And Bob was not one to sit on a thought.

Backed by his friend and mentor Peter Drucker—that Peter Drucker, intellectual titan of the modern business corporation—Bob began to plot the second half of his life and career. He took profile tests.

He hired a renowned business coach. He researched, read, consulted more experts, adapted business theories, and wrestled with hard questions. In the end, at Peter's urging, he published his trail of blood in a book he called *Halftime: Moving from Success to Significance*.

It crawled out of the gate. And then a few people read it and handed it on. After a while, men and women who'd never heard of Bob were ordering his book by the box to hand off to their friends all asking the same "Is this all there is?" questions. Through the next twenty-five years, a book about finding significance became a million-seller, multiplying through lives like mine and stories like this one.

## MY ADULT VERSION OF "I AM THIRD"

GOD IS FIRST: Be an authentic follower of Jesus. "Love the Lord your God with all your heart and with all your soul and with all your mind. This is the first and greatest commandment." Matthew 22:37–38

OTHERS ARE SECOND: Be a godly family man and neighbor. "And the second is like it: 'Love your neighbor as yourself.' All the Law and the Prophets hang on these two commandments." Matthew 22:39–40

I AM THIRD: Be a wise leader in God's eyes. "But the wisdom that comes from heaven is first of all pure; then peace-loving, considerate, submissive, full of mercy and good fruit, impartial and sincere." James 3:17

## A HALFTIME BY ANY OTHER NAME

*Halftime* refers obviously to the break in the game to review strategy and tactics. It may be a scheduled halftime or unexpected—an injury, maybe. Maybe the other team is running away with the game. Whatever the reason, the game isn't over.

Stephen Covey famously said to start with the end in mind, and that's the point in a time-out or halftime. I remember when I learned to think through what my win would look like.

12

"When you die," the speaker had said to my semicircle of career refugees, "you have an exam of just two questions: 'What did you do about Jesus? And what did you do with the gifts God gave you?'"

Down a dusty corridor in my brain that day, I felt gears groan and shudder. For decades I'd put off thinking about life because I could. Now my mind swept back to my senior year in high school, to my early decisions and the "I am third" values. I thought of losing my father and finding God. I thought of my career, its end, and the surprise of finding myself with no plan.

What should I do with the gifts God gave me? And by the way, what were the gifts?

## GREATEST PAIN, GREATEST JOY

One morning in the conference, our facilitator broke us into pairs. He told us to name our greatest joy and greatest pain as potential clues to our callings. A woman who became pregnant as an unmarried teen had built homes and programs to help girls in similar crises. One man had turned his love of sports into an entire baseball league for inner-city kids.

That morning I paired off with Bob. My greatest joy, I told him, was my young daughter, Grace, on her champion saddlebred. My joy was seeing her joy. My greatest pain: Dad's sudden and unexpected death. He was in his mid-sixties, healthy, an active former Marine. He also was, from a bad wartime experience, an avoider of doctors. Dad died in a December, and for the rest of that winter emptiness overtook me. By spring I was in a church. Bob nodded. His father had died before he was ten years old. His only child, Ross, died tragically as a young adult.

Back in the larger group, each of us summarized our partner's answers. All Bob said was, "When Randy's earthly father died, he turned to his heavenly father," but the words fell on me like poetry. My uncertainty, instead of pushing me to the margins, drew understanding.

Only a day before, my group had a whiteboard exercise to draw our future, no words allowed. I drew a bad sketch of a dollar sign and a cross. Afterwards, standing next to it, I saw Bob's eyes light up. He knew the tug between meaning and money.

A story goes with that. In Bob's work to get from success to significance, he once hired a consultant and proceeded to unload onto him a mountain of confusion. All of it. For hours. Exhausted, the consultant grabbed a legal pad and drew a box on it. "Your box can only hold one thing," he told Bob. "A dollar sign or a cross. You decide." That was the choice Bob saw in me now.

At this point, you may be thinking that God in your box would be a one-way ticket to missionary work in Africa. But if I'm right, you're wrong.

I'm telling you that God in your box is your ticket to peace, to the work you're made for. He knows you better than you know yourself. Your biggest regret will be having waited to do it. "Our hearts are restless until they find their rest in you," Saint Augustine wrote. You're not called to the end of the world, only to the end of yourself, where God hands you the best version of yourself.

In my case, after twenty-five years in a family-controlled company, the time came in 2009 for me to go, ending decades-long relationships. The discontent in me wasn't new; I'd seen the signs. But leaving was hard. Even then, with the pain had come an unexpected sense of gratitude for the years, the resources, the experiences, even for the timing of my exit. The postrecession era of 2009 was a window to diversify out of ag holdings into the broader stock market. Financially, God gave me solid footing.

## DRAWING ON THE FUTURE

*"You have fifteen minutes to draw a picture of your ideal future. No words allowed."*

Back to that morning at the whiteboard with instructions to draw our dream for work and life. No talking; nothing spelled out. And the clock was ticking.

What would you draw? As I described earlier, I sketched a tall cross, its base in the soil, its top in the clouds. To its left, I drew a dollar sign for the marketplace and my finances. To its right, I drew a heart, signifying relationships and philanthropy. Where the two planks met, I put a bull's-eye. On the vertical plank, clouds to earth, I imagined a line of interconnected hands.

Every detail mattered to me. I'm no artist, but gut sense is a strong suit from my trading years when decisions ran ahead of rationale. Now again free of words, my drawing linked finance and philanthropy to a future where business meets nonprofit and to a generational handoff connecting this world to eternity.

That simple sketch would take years to fully unpack, but its existence was a milestone. In a few mind-blowing minutes, my head had gotten a chance to catch up with my instincts.

That was game-changer number one. Number two, as simplistic as it sounds, was the idea of harmony. In my career, my strengths centered on "strategic vision," on planning, resources, and positive influence—always as separate considerations. I could lead groups to consider their personal lives, their community involvement, their philanthropies—but separately, never as three parts of one overriding purpose.

Once, years earlier, our family attorney had confronted—I mean, challenged—my wife, Debbie, and me to improve our giving style. We shotgunned, he said. We were all goodwill and no good aim. And here we were at it again. Until my interests, work, values, investments, relationships . . . all served a single purpose, any one of them could undo the whole.

## THE GROUPS WHO HELPED ME DREAM

The whiteboard exercise, sending us to somewhere pre-verbal, is a trick to get unstuck. Another trick is to think about groups you've been in. Stay with me.

In my life, three different groups have helped me calibrate my dreams. In your life, think of teams you've been on, work groups, clubs. Even now, for me to go forward, it helps me to go back to why I joined and what I gained. In college the team was my fraternity. At the end of my career, I had an organization of peers. Since midlife, it's been the church. In certain groups, our roles can help us consider the people we admire and put words to what motivates us.

FarmHouse Fraternity, with its motto "Builders of Men," came into my life when I was a sophomore at Kansas State University. At dinner, in study hall, shooting hoops, I'd hear about someone, some hobby or interest, some challenge or achievement, and my standards would inch up. Several guys had overcome hardships just to get to KSU. Some were stars in their majors. The fraternity's vision inspired me. As an alumnus on the FarmHouse Foundation Board of Trustees, I helped it set up a fund and a campaign to advocate for the national bone marrow registry. Another time I helped set up matching funds for international travel. Being part of that group made me think big ideas were possible, and each time the ROI overpaid me.

The Halftime Institute gave me a set of iron-on-iron peers. Many leaders in a single group can devolve into posturing and competition, but this group was all students and all teachers. I came to it needing to rethink my life; I got a brain trust of people enough like me for me to feel understood, but sufficiently different to stretch my world. Several of us remain close.

The church is in the fabric of my life everywhere in the world I go. Its constancy and influence, and the astonishing tapestry of people in the body of Christ, expose me to truths I could come to no other way. As the church helps me define meaning and purpose, it elevates my dreams.

———————

Not everyone is a "joiner," but groups bring benefits impossible to anticipate. A man I know heard a professor speak and signed up for the prof's class in a neighboring city. The topic was obscure, the class was small, the drive was long—and my friend ended up attending for two decades. People otherwise off his radar became like family. He read Plato, Aristotle, and authors he couldn't have previously pronounced. The Thursday night discussions, he says, full of robust disagreement and mutual regard, taught him to think.

Another friend, who is white, began attending church on Sunday mornings with her one Black friend. The music, the energy, the sermons were thrilling. She also felt painfully conspicuous. For weeks she had to will herself to walk through the parking lot and in the front door. But important things were astir. Now in the minority, she got to know her brothers and sisters in Christ in their world, not hers. At various times in a Sunday morning service, the entire congregation held hands to pray for each other. Some days those prayers left her in tears. Before long, her conversations about race were informed by love.

How much time do you have? A friend's granddaughter, just out of college, joined a scholastic cruise to the Middle East, Russia, and former Soviet countries. For eight months she saw world sites with top teachers and fellow learners. Like former soldiers or a sports team, she and her fellow travelers forever share once-in-a-lifetime moments. She reads international headlines now keenly aware that another country is someone else's backyard.

Groups, groups, groups. A group can be spin class, Meals on Wheels, AA, mission trips, continuing education, marathon training, a cooking or photography club. In my life, no single group ever gave me full direction, but every group gave me more than I could have guessed.

Tap every opportunity around you. Whatever you're feeling as you begin this book—if you're uneasy or bored, if something in you wants more but you can't articulate why or how—you're in a good place and in good company. Your feelings are normal. Whoever you are, if you've come to the "Why am I restless?" or "Who should I be?" questions, my response is, "Are you ready?"

Say yes, and let's get to it.

## ASK YOURSELF

1. Growing up, what did I dream of becoming?

2. When I lose myself in the pleasure of a task, what am I doing?

3. These days, when I let myself dream, where does my mind go?

4. If I were free to do anything—if nothing stood in my way—what would I do?

5. What groups, past or present, have affected my life, and why?

## WHAT IS SMOLDERING DISCONTENT?

1. **You feel restless.** Something's out of sync. Maybe you can name it, maybe not. But something has to change.

2. **You want more.** More joy, more peace, more fulfillment. Your life looks fine, but you're low on inspiration, low on knowing God, low in self-regard.

3. **You lack meaning.** By now you expected to feel better about your life. You sense that your knowledge, skills, relationships, and talents could do more, affect more people. Maybe you know where you can pour your unique gifts into new passions, maybe not.

4. **You long not just to finish but to finish well.** You think more about your legacy.

5. **You're overdue to put first things first.** For years, you hit delay on family, God, community. Now you want people and other priorities in the right order.

— Adapted from Rhonda Kehlbeck, The Halftime Institute

**CHAPTER TWO**

# LEARN TO PRAY

*This Day and in Eternity*

"When you pray, do not be like the hypocrites . . ."

**— Jesus, Matthew 5:6**

The first prayer I remember is one my father would say easy as an exhale. *Grant that we grow more like to thee, this day and in eternity.*

It's a line from a poem, that much I know, and for Dad that was the sum of it. Thomas Linville, by the time I arrived, was a World War II vet, the son of a World War I vet, and a farmer in southwest Kansas. He'd studied education in college, then traded textbooks and classrooms for wheat in the summer, corn and milo in the fall. In cold months he worked feeder cattle on winter wheat pastures. He was resolute and gentle, shrewd and plainspoken. He provided for his family and put four kids through college. Political correctness would have been foreign to him.

Dad's prayer comes to me in scenes of morning drives to change the irrigation. Or in the truck as he slowed along a fence, or as we moved through chores. In my head, always in his cadence, I hear his simplicity and trust.

The words stayed obscure to me, though, until much later in my life, typical of kids and parents. Dad left us as I was building a family and carving a career down a narrow line. In those years, talking to God was like improvising a speech to some unseen dignitary in front of people who assumed I knew him. I'd string together a few clichés, bless the cooks, and sign off.

## LEARNING HOW TO PRAY

Then two things rocked my world. The first was in December 1991, when Dad's unexpected heart attack blew a canyon-sized hole in the family and imploded my center of gravity. The second was a few months later, in early spring, '92, when a church draped its welcome banner across the entrance of a nearby funeral home.

In retrospect, I cherish the timing of that banner. Services in a funeral home took some adjusting, but Debbie and I both felt drawn, and we found ourselves in a small starter congregation. In those days, the senior pastor could still drop by with a newcomer's mug, which he must have kept in the back seat of his car by the case. The 'burbs were teeming with cultural Christians like Debbie and me, full of unmet hungers.

As we involved ourselves, I served on the operations committee, helping manage the church's white-knuckle growth. Our first year of Sundays may have drawn fewer than two hundred people, but in the next decade, the congregation would swell and spill into five campuses with twenty-two thousand people.

We'd been members for several years, and Debbie was out of town one Sunday, when I said to myself, "I go to church and I'm spiritually empty." That morning at a recruitment table in a hallway I signed us up for a five-year discipleship study. If reading the entire Bible in twelve months seemed ambitious, and it did, little did I anticipate that inside that year I'd also be praying publicly.

Tuesday evenings a dozen middle-aged spiritual freshmen like me found seats in the lower level of a home built like a villa. Our leader had lost his wife and daughter in a car accident; his faith was tested and deep. Every week he assigned us reading, and every week, to close, he'd ask us for our joys and concerns. And one of us would be asked to pray. Out loud. Alone. Personal updates were fine with me, but the public piety thing put ice in my veins. I felt unqualified, unworthy. All of us did.

But that's where I began to talk to God and to learn the protocols of prayer. Never mind eloquence; God wants our hearts. Thank him. Tell him you love him. Confess when you mess up. Ask for his help. Pray for others.

And we flailed, we stammered, and we found our way. By the time I could pray with others, I was also praying on my own.

Getting to know God within a group, by the way, made sense to me, as the rest of this book will bear out. In school and sports, in livestock judging, in farm work . . . every personal advance has come to me within a team. Businesses have their departments, account groups, committees, subcommittees, think tanks, you name it. And some industry outfits are wildly impressive. But only in faith groups did I encounter the high-performance unity of imperfect people all raising each other.

To be clear, Christians are human, and humans are fallen. No Christian group offers perfection or sinlessness. I'm simply saying when the starting line is shared values, the finish line moves up. It seems to shorten the run, and the runners spur each other.

## THE DISCIPLINES OF SPONTANEOUS PRAYER

Now a confession. As I grew in faith, when someone asked me to pray or I said I would, within minutes my good intentions had scattered like leaves in an autumn gust. Over time, observing certain believers who were serious about prayer, I learned to do three things.

1. When I said I'd pray, I prayed right then and there.

2. Once I'd prayed, I'd make physical notes to follow up. And I would follow up.

3. Eventually, as I describe in the next section, I formed a prayer team.

"Right then" is what it says. In the car, the gym, a hallway, in the way my dad kept prayer as close as breath, I'd silently go to God. After that, as soon as I could, often on a phone app, I'd put that person or problem on a list under one of the four life categories I wanted to keep in harmony: community, personal, marketplace, or philanthropy.

There's more. From the guilty soil of forgetting to pray for people who asked sprung prayers for scores of people who'd never ask. Even for politicians because we're told to pray for people in authority and because the Holy Spirit can work through anyone. I'd pray, "Let them be public servants and statesmen first."

By now you may be thinking, *Commitments, deadlines, lists, categories: What happened to his dad's simple prayer?* My response is that prayer is natural but it also rewards routine. A set time to pray, a book or outline to structure your thoughts, a conversation with God through the day . . . all build relationship. Our disciplines, as we acquire them, help us draw near our Father, stay attuned to his work, and become more like him.

## PRAYER AND A BOOK OF LIFE

So should prayer have structure? Regardless of the answer, my nature seeks it, and I'm more consistent for it.

The structure I use came by trial and error, copy and paste. At the writing of this book, in a typical week of mornings, I pray in a sequence called ACTS: adoration, confession, thanksgiving, supplication. In the supplication (asking) phase, I pray through my four categories, closing with, "Lord, what's the most important thing for me today?"

A word about records. In what we do for others, the bottom line is not profit or numbers. The bottom line is changed lives. As a former business executive, I lived by profit and numbers. The "changed lives" criteria was a shock, but eventually I created a system. For years now my yardstick has been my *Book of Life*, weekly updates of my prayers, projects, and priorities. Sunday mornings as I call up and survey that week's prayer list, I open my *Book of Life* and ask: *What was going on last week? What's up for this week? What still has me worried or stumped?* I write summaries, make notes, and pray.

"Sweet hour of prayer" is more than mere sentiment. As I consider a person or a problem before God, knots slacken and anxieties lose steam. A great wall of priorities, projects, and networking pressure dissolves to reveal doorways. Like a crop cycle or a corporate year, in those thirty to ninety minutes on Sundays, I see my days and the people in them advance, resolve, improve. I see lives and circumstances change by degrees. Certainly I change. Day by day, person by person, routine prayer and regular review help me see God's love and want to stay in his will.

Nothing comes overnight, but much comes with consistency. If prayer in your life is sporadic, too often initiated in fear, mostly transactional ("If you give me X, I promise Y"), an easy first step is just to pray the Lord's Prayer every day. No matter what. Pray for five minutes—a minute of silence in his presence, a short read, and a prayer.

"Daily?" you ask. "Doesn't the repetition get old?"

Good question, because for me, all repetition is suspect. *Is this task redundant?* I'll ask myself. *Could someone else do it and my time be more efficient?* The answer is that prayer gets old the way nutrition and sleep get old. Even on the days it feels like the last thing we want or have time for, it feeds and sustains us.

So you start simply. A journal or notebook, a scrapbook, a prayer ledger, notes on your phone, the back of an envelope. You set markers to remember, adapt, and grow, and to be thankful.

"I am the vine; you are the branches," Jesus told his disciples. "If you remain in me and I in you, you will bear much fruit; apart from me you can do nothing. . . . As the Father has loved me, so have I loved you. Now remain in my love" (John 15:5, 9).

We stay with it because prayer is the habit that forms us.

## A COMMUNITY OF PRAYER

The idea to form a group for prayer came in the first year of the five-year Bible study. In the joys-and-concerns section of a meeting, moved by certain people, I'd take note. "Would you be part of a small group for specific prayers?" I'd ask afterwards, one on one. Years later, a team of some dozen people—several of them out of state now—still pray for parts of my "community, personal, marketplace, philanthropy" spread. And I pray for them. Better than Facebook, we remain connected by what matters.

And we learn from each other. That they would teach me, I expected. That it ran both ways was a surprise. After I sent out a quarterly email prayer list, I might hear, "It's instructive you put X in your request," or "The way you thank God helps me."

God can use anything. For my part, to take the time to write a prayer on paper, or type it on a screen, is to see it as a real thing, no longer a shapeless longing or vague fear.

Prayer is not rocket science or only for the initiated, yet it changes lives and worlds. And any system beats no system. The simple prayer list below is mine, shown here from a regular letter to my prayer team. Because it helped me, each section opens with lines from Seth Barnes's book *Listening Prayer*.

**PERSONAL:** *Is my walk with you authentic? As I tell you my heart, help me listen to you. Help me judge less, forgive more, love freely.*

Guide Jake to grow spiritually, find his calling and fields of study, and remain open to the Spirit. Guide Grace in following Jesus, loving family, teaching preschool, and loving saddlebreds. Help Mom use her care network for best health in the balance of her years.

**COMMUNITY:** *Bless us with discernment, favor, guidance, and wisdom.*

The book: bless the editing and cowriting to fully develop life and business concepts for your use. Church: guide our leadership and the fall Crossroads workshop.

**MARKETPLACE:** *As I work in the market, help me lead wisely in your eyes.*

Investments: guide our plans to steward family resources for a godly lifestyle and legacy.

Triquetra: give us discernment, favor, guidance, and wisdom to unite the right team of teams.

**PHILANTHROPY:** *What does a closer walk with you look like? Am I walking in the right direction?*

Global Scholars: bless the sending program and new society of Christian scholars. Halftime Institute: praise for the life and legacy of founder Bob Buford; continued success of all programs.

## THE HABIT THAT SHAPES US

Is it possible you've come to your own cross-in-the-box moment—a choice between God and something else, however good it is? You can wait to choose until you're desperate, and desperate times will come, but why put off the peace?

My moment came when I had to harmonize the many parts of my life under a single heading. In writing. I had to show that instead of a loosely connected series of random acts, my days had a single encompassing reason and aim. My only way forward was to commit wildly, fully to God. And when I finally did, of all things, what came to my mind was Dad's prayer.

*Grant that we grow more like to thee, this day and in eternity.*

## THE ACTS PRAYER

*Any prayer structure helps a person get off the ground. I still use this one.*

**ADORATION:** God "inhabits the praises of his people." When we begin by addressing him with terms like "wonderful counselor," "almighty God," "creator of the universe," we hit reset in ourselves. In the light of his glory and love, we mix awe and a child's favor with a loving parent.

**CONFESSION:** To repent is to identify and turn from anything keeping us from God. Why not do it? God knows us better than we know ourselves, and no sin can trump his grace. We unload the worst, then bask in his forgiveness and love.

**THANKSGIVING:** Gratitude has uncanny power. As we thank God for big things, for the minutiae, for hard things, and for his answers to other prayers, our spirits soar. Really.

**SUPPLICATION:** Pray for your leaders—the ones you despise, the ones you vote for. Pray for the people you lead or influence. Pray as people ask you to and pray for those who never ask. Pray as any person comes to mind. Our prayers for others shape us too.

# ASK YOURSELF

1. What is my honest opinion of prayer?

2. Does anything about prayer scare me?

3. Have I ever given it a real try? If not, why do I put it off?

4. When people ask me to pray for them, what do I feel, and what do I do?

5. If every good intention came true, what would prayer in my life look like?

**CHAPTER THREE**

# INNOVATE

*Old Steps, New Dance*

"Innovation distinguishes between
a leader and a follower."

— **Steve Jobs**

Every summer come July, my family trades the Kansas humidity and heat for Beaver Creek, Colorado, where the Rockies sprout with Midwesterners like us, along with the Texans and sundry other climate tourists.

Some of them are artists. One year in downtown Beaver Creek, across from our lodge, the Vilar Performing Arts Center hosted Savion Glover, modern wonder of the centuries-old thrill of tap dance. After a few opening footwork pyrotechnics, as the audience members picked up their chins, he ran a large overhead video of his giants: Bojangles Robinson, the Nicholas Brothers . . . Fred Astaire. While they danced and dazzled above us, Glover duplicated their dazzle onstage.

And then before our eyes, as he mimicked his legends, we saw every step become his own. "I take from the masters," he told us, "and repackage in my own sell."

And right there, to a fascinatin' rhythm, Savion Glover was innovation: old steps looking all-new. Innovators don't create; they creatively change, improve, and adapt. And in the right shoes, for all the world, it looks like genius. Gregory Hines, another dance legend, called Savion Glover maybe the best tap dancer ever.

The question for us is, *Where do we get our steps?* If growth is change and nothing is new under the sun, where do we get our ideas? What stirs our need to imitate? What compels us to grab a pen or our cell phone to take notes?

Per Savion Glover, I submit that what keeps us on our toes, throughout our lives, is the best of all that's around us and all that's come before.

# AN INVITATION TO INNOVATION

Life is innovation. By imitation or by contrast, every one of us is an amalgam of the influence of our parents, family, friends, communities, and more. Far-off leaders, next-door neighbors, and the person (or persons) we marry all affect us. Our thoughts mirror or challenge our teachers, preachers, coaches, professors, peers, coworkers, and times. We are decisions we've come to, the downtime we fill, the places we happen on or find by GPS. We're the sports we may overindulge in, the books we read, the television or online shows we spend too much time watching. Our lives bear the unseen imprints of groups, prayers, experiences, and encounters.

Each one of us is a testament to selective creation, knowingly or not, from a cosmos of neighbors, events, surroundings, and ideas. And all of it is innovation.

When I retired from the ag industry and finally set up a fitness routine, I innovated. Like too many of us, I'd let myself believe that a workout would poach from my personal or work time. But what daunted me was someone else's idea of a workout. The point of innovation is make an idea work for me, my way.

At age fifty-five I started with Pilates to begin to move again. For cardio, I folded in walking. Gym time with a friend, a yoga class, tennis dates, online instruction—we find what works, and one thing spurs a next thing. In Pilates I gravitated to equipment. As exercise grew routine and my energy rose, I improved my diet, which became another patchwork of ideas. Not every notion or exercise or recipe fits every one of us, but when something fits, we make it ours.

My spiritual innovation started with a guest speaker at church teaching the disciplines of Bible reading, prayer, and accountability. I knew I needed more, and this man had the goods. In a Savion Glover moment—seeing a master I wanted to imitate—I grabbed a pen to adapt his ideas into my daily routines.

My first devotional was something from Pastor Eugene Peterson. Warming to what I read, each day I'd paraphrase his writing into my own takeaways. As my reading list grew, the paraphrasing dropped off. But I'd still copy a sentence or highlight a phrase thinking, *Yes, or That's what I wrestle with.* More selection, more innovation.

These days, every day, I download a half-dozen devotions onto a single Android page and harvest:

- **The YouVersion of the Holy Bible** pushes out a daily Scripture; a ticker shows how many days I read for classic Type-A motivation.

- **Alistair Begg's** *Truth for Life* abounds with plainspoken, clear-minded, and Scottish-accented insights.

- **GoTandem.com** started with a Christian techie who believes we need the Bible a certain number of times a week. The app learns my interests, spiritual needs, and weak points; in my dips in the day, it texts an uplifting message.

- **BillyGraham.org's** daily missives speak to me. Growing up, I dismissed Graham as a fire-and-brimstone guy. Now I know him as a thought leader.

- **BibleGateway.com**, an online Bible, daily dishes a verse with links to related chapters and verses or to multiple translations. Some tool.

We open our minds to what's out there and narrow to what works for us. Physically, spiritually, name the category . . . gleaning from sources we find, we innovate and up our games.

## BUILDING ON OTHERS' WORDS

When I left grad school, my master's in economics got me into trading, the gritty work of moving agricultural goods through the supply chain. When that went well, I was bumped up to management, which is more complex than trading and comes with no instructions.

Short on attention and tight on time, I grabbed a book—in this case, a thin volume called *The One Minute Manager*. In my generation, this was a star business book, and from that day on, when I came across anything by the author, Ken Blanchard, I'd buy, read, and innovate.

Professionally, we all want a library shelf of first-rate resources. If you asked me today to name my main management book, I'd cross my study and pull out *Leadership and the One Minute Manager.* In essence, it says that authority is never one-size-fits-all and then explains how authority works.

As a respected voice in American business, Ken Blanchard became a master on my overhead screen. Then one day in 2010, at a meeting of a board I'd joined, I found myself three chairs from Ken's wife, Dr. Margie Blanchard. Quick, brilliant, wise, she and Ken became the virtuoso tap duo to my Footwork 101. When they joined the rest of us for post-meeting dinners, the innovating hit high gear. Ken would get us on some management or leadership topic, press the pedal, and off we'd go, men and women on the front lines of current business issues, reveling in a master class of management, leadership, decision-making, and more. For most of us, these conversations surfaced wisdom good for the very next day.

Somewhere in that abundance of dance steps, I acquired the habit of hoarding. "Hoard" sounds harsh. "Stockpile," maybe. "Collect and list" would be too tame. I came upon the practice in a book that drew from Jesus as the greatest leadership role model of all time. Toward the end of the book, the author lists his emergency numbers.

The numbers refer to Bible verses, and if that seems gratuitous, you've spent too little time under fire. Beneath headings like "Fear and Repentance" and "Guidance" was four-alarm aid like Psalm 23 (ESV) ("though I walk through the valley of the shadow of death"); 1 John 1:9 ("If we confess our sins, he is faithful and just and will forgive us our sins and purify us from all unrighteousness"); and Proverbs 3:5–6 (NKJV) ("lean not on your own understanding. In all your ways acknowledge Him, and He shall direct your paths").

How did I innovate? Given the value of these timeless words and my admiration for great people and top-shelf wisdom, I put together my version of emergency numbers, a stash that would take on its own life.

Who can explain the power of words? In a speech or a book, across a dinner table, from a parchment fifteen hundred years old, words can still give life or death. (Think of words you hold onto from a parent or authority figure, or words you wanted to hear and never did.)

In the way Savion Glover studied his masters and mastered his art, in the way I was fortunate to read, innovate, and even meet some of the authors I admired, we master in our masters. We find what sharpens and feeds us and store it up for ready reference.

At the back of this book, I've put my treasury of wisdom, words that at some point left the page and lifted my life. And still do. With every reading, which is often, I again draw energy. I think I always will because after any meal, however nutritious, a person eventually needs to refill.

## BUILD ON THE CURVE

Maybe you've heard of the sigmoid curve, the life cycle of almost everything. On a business graph the curve looks like a capital S on its side: a dip, an uptrend, a decline. Wikipedia, that august authority, explains the idea's mathematics. But that actual curve—the dip, growth, and drop-off—reflects all of life.

In the marketplace the sigmoid curve affirms that every product or service has a beginning, middle, and end. Smart companies work with that. Before a product or service runs its course, another has hit the floor running. You'd think that would be obvious. But plenty of companies miss the curve, as in the famous Polaroid case. When the market for camera film died, Polaroid had no more ideas, and a global brand, a household name, declared bankruptcy. In contrast, when society pulled the cord on rotary phones, AT&T quickly reinvented itself as not a phone business but a communications company, and it lives on.

When I became CEO, our outside planning expert, Dr. Jon Hope of Rockhurst University, taught by the sigmoid curve. Every business in our company identified its lifespan dynamics and set our objectives by them. We might come up with new ideas, or we might find ourselves at a cycle's end. On the irreducible sequence from identify to develop, optimize, mature, close, we could invent as necessary and avoid as possible. Mathematics can't begin to capture all the sigmoid curve has to teach.

How does the sigmoid curve work for you? Across every person's daily life runs a beginning here, growth there, somewhere an end. As one comes to a close, you draw ideas from every source necessary. You combine and adapt to your life, and you start something new. For me, part of drawing from every source necessary is to consult the wisdom of men and women ahead of me on the curve.

*In the parts we become whole.* Your life, your existence, filled with beginnings and ends, is your wide-open invitation to constantly innovate and consistently adapt. In the spirit of Savion Glover, you gather and build on the best of what's come before.

You curate, innovate, and dance.

## ASK YOURSELF

1. What people, places, or things form my amalgam?

2. When have I conspicuously copied or adapted from someone or modeled myself after someone?

3. Have I ever saved a quote or thought? Why? What did I do with it? Where is it now?

4. If we all are amalgams of people and influences around us, how does that create opportunities for me?

5. Where in my life can I identify beginnings, middles, and ends? How does doing that help me plan?

# RESOLVE

**CHAPTER FOUR**

# CHOOSE

*God's Will and Your Call*

"Whether I hear God's call or not depends on
the condition of my ears, and exactly what I
hear depends upon my spiritual attitude."

**— Oswald Chambers**

W hen our son, Jake, was in college, he'd changed majors twice already when he came to Debbie and me with news of another change. Like his buddies at school, he was ready to trust his instincts and keep moving. "It feels right," he told us that night, followed by the seemingly airtight, "It's a God thing."

I know the rock-like certainty of a strong feeling. Like Jake, I grew up with a will and with a sense that to want something badly made it right. I've also done a lot of living since then. "Some feelings we want to trust and verify," I said to Jake that night, "to be sure it's a God thing and not just a Jake thing."

Because my son knows his dad, he crossed his legs and sat back. I reached for my cell phone to type in "Alpha Course Five CSs."

The Alpha Course is an eleven-week film series used by churches worldwide to invite believers and nonbelievers to explore faith. Part of its tool kit is a powerhouse of a little checklist for decision-making: "The Five CSs," a three-way of facts, personal perspectives, and Scripture.

I believe in gut sense, but big decisions call for reason too. If the choice were ice cream flavors, Jake's feelings would rule the day. For school, spouse, majors, careers—with no obvious rights or wrongs— he needed to both trust and verify.

Because God gives us spirits and minds.

## THE ART OF GOOD DECISIONS

First, a qualifier. I've never heard God's voice. Not audibly. A divine mystery is defined as two truths that on the surface seem to contradict each other. Into that category I put how God speaks: no voice, and yet we hear him.

Sometimes what we hear is his silence. Author Brennan Manning told of a brilliant ethicist unsettled in his vocation. For several months the man served in Calcutta with Mother Teresa, and one day he asked her to pray for him. Would she ask for God to give him clarity? The founder of the Sisters of Charity, the Nobel Prize recipient, the icon with, it would seem, her own hotline to God, turned down the request. "I never had clarity," she said. "I only had trust. I will pray that you trust God."

From my decades of belief, in the quest to know God's will, give me Mother Teresa's informed trust over cloud formations, voices, or Morgan Freeman's drop-ins in *Bruce Almighty*. God is the shaper of souls, the perfecter of our faith; he speaks in his time and his way, never in a cliché, never in means we can manufacture or manipulate.

In our conversation with Jake that night, Debbie and I went through the checklist below: a balance of inner sense, common sense, and Scripture. If you're facing a decision right now, you might read it with that in mind.

1. **Commanding Scripture:** Is there a clear biblical command or directive? In cases of dating another man's wife or walking a hotel bill, see Exodus 20. Jake's college major fell in the personal judgment zone.

2. **Compelling spirit:** Do you have a strong sense? Jake had a vibe, he told us, and God's will certainly may include a vibe, but the reverse is not true. A feeling does not confirm a call from God.

3. **Common sense:** What part of your decision turns on reason? Have you assessed the pros and cons? Likely consequences? Had Jake talked to anyone in his proposed new major? Was he factoring in his own temperament, personality, and natural skills?

4. **The counsel of saints:** Have you talked to people whose thinking you respect? Seldom did my father discourage me on anything, but as I was leaving high school, he told me to hang up my track shoes and focus on studies. He knew I wanted to coach. He knew my studies came easily and that I worked hard at athletics. A little harshly, I thought, he said to me, "Coaches are a dime a dozen, but with your mind you can do something special." That was my counsel of saints, my answer to "What do your friends and advisors say?" The postscript to Dad's veto is that what I loved about sports was the teamwork, the challenges, helping people find and use their strengths. Turns out I did coach. Over and over. Just no jerseys.

5. **Circumstantial signs:** Are you coming to walls or to doors? Or to surprises? (How many times do we chase a deal or some person only to catch something different and better?) Our family has learned that dead ends turn our attention to new vistas. Where we used to feel disappointment or see a coincidence, now we ask, "Where's God in this?"

"Expect the unexpected" is sound advice. As a Christian looking for God's will—as a person who too often tries to create the circumstances that I think I want—my counsel now is not just to expect the unexpected, but to respect it. *Respect the unexpected.*

By that I mean God is in the letdowns, the surprises, the disappointments, the unplanned, and the out-of-the-blue. You're trying to adopt, and you get pregnant. You interview for a job, and they offer you one unadvertised. A failing grade forces you to retake a class with a new teacher who "gets" you. Never underestimate God.

## THE MEEKNESS TO LEARN

*Where do we see God at work?* The first time someone opened a meeting with that question, my face must have gone blank. Wasn't God at work everywhere? Or more to the point, who can know? Eventually, I'd learn to look for places where God is turning over ground and planting, and to identify the harvest in changed lives.

I'd also learn that God's work in a specific area doesn't necessarily make it my calling. But to know that, I'd have to ask questions. I'd have to test and evaluate. And yes, those things take time because they multiply trial and error. But in God's economy no effort is wasted—especially when, in humility, we look for and allow him to lead.

I once joined a board and at our first meeting learned we actually were two groups. One was business executives pursuing the double bottom line of for-profit work and ministry. The other was pastors wanting to hone their executive skills. And there we all were: top evangelical influencers, their business-world counterparts, and yours truly.

That first meeting opened with a devotion. The next devotion, a voice of authority said, was my turn. My fellow board members were giants, and I felt woefully underqualified, but I had notebooks, and

RESOLVE

I went to them for ideas. In the very first one, I came to Jesus saying, "The meek will inherit the earth."

Ahh, "meek." For years I'd see the word in the Beatitudes and press the gas. Humility, I got. Mercy, kindness, selflessness, sacrifice—all terms I thought I understood. But weakness? "Blessed are the wimpy"? Why would Jesus say that?

Then came the day when I learned that "meek" means just the opposite of wimpy. It means "strength in submission," the mission of both of the boards.

At our next meeting, I opened my devotion with, "Picture a stallion submissive to his rider's touch." Around the table, I sent a photo of petite Grace at a horse show, her animal's massive spirit docile to a bridle and bit. "This is how we make our way to God's way," I said. "Subject to his lead, we look for answers not out of our own power or vision but, in meekness, submitted to his."

## "IS GOD'S WORK MY WORK TOO?"

To test whether a "God project" might be my project too, I learned to use low-cost probes, also known as trying on work for size. Typically, the probes were with organizations familiar to me. I either know someone in the nonprofit or someone who did.

To start, I'd try to build a relationship with someone in the group to help me understand its vision, to see if I shared it. If that clicked, I had a filter—a checklist—worked out ahead of time.

As a strategist I'd attempt to gauge attitude, aptitude, and resources for what the group needed to succeed. Then I'd ask if the organization was healthy, strong, and receptive. Some answers came in financial statements, some in reputation, some in conversation. If all answers were yes, I'd ask how I might be a catalyst to help. Seldom did the stars align, but when they did, I'd do the *next* thing: I'd ask to volunteer for a limited term.

Usually I'd help with a project, a new direction, and let things naturally evolve. In that period, I'd assess the quality of relationships, the amount of trust, and the group's need for my skill set. Our time together might last six months or a decade. If it went nowhere, better to know sooner than later.

Well and good, you say, but how do you know what nonprofit work to try on?

You start with yourself. Remember, I built a career on moving farm products from seed to pantry shelf, work that was geographically diverse but highly repetitive. How would I know what other work to explore? How does anyone know?

I went back to my interests and passions. "What passions?" After years of motivating other people, many of us lose touch with *any* passion. That was me. Plus, the strengths I'd needed for specialized ag supply chain—my abilities to assess, strategize, and guide others— were general. Everything about me was general, which seemed problematic.

Until I saw that general skills can have broad uses.

My low-cost probes—my volunteer projects—became less about matching my skills than matching my interest. I knew I could bring strategy and vision. Instead of looking for a position, I looked at groups and nonprofits for their services and directions. When one caught my eye, as I said, I'd study it online, consult my friends (or friends of friends), and set up a meeting. If a door opened, I'd volunteer. If doors seemed to stick, I'd move on.

Alpha USA, a group I admire, didn't need me. My probe told me so. First, I attended the group's national gathering. A few months later, in Chicago, I met with leaders from London, world headquarters for its 130 countries. Its mission to take Jesus into the marketplace of ideas fit my interests, but my skills fell outside their needs. I remain a fan.

About that time a friend linked me to the World Soy Foundation (WSF), which was waging war on malnutrition, a problem more widespread and insidious than hunger. WSF had soymilk processing units in Central America and Africa. This time doors swung open. For several years, and with great pleasure, I lent strategy to its rapidly expanding programs.

Along the way I learned about Global Scholars Society (GS), which trains and sends Christian-minded academics into developing countries and nations off the grid. I helped them launch a multilayered means to connect, train, and support Christian academics already in universities, then I left the board.

Of a baker's dozen probes, six in some way took and others fell along a spectrum. As Grace was leaving high school, she and I came across Adventures in Missions (AIM), which sends twentysomethings around the world. Grace moved on this time, but founder Seth Barnes and I hit it off, and I stayed on as his informal strategic advisor. AIM runs on services and donations, and for eighteen months I helped tighten operations for both.

The sigmoid curve reminds us that a calling, too, has a beginning, middle, and end. Part of knowing our callings, and a reason for this book, is that a time also comes for us to leave. With each board I joined, for the length of my service, I knew it was my purpose. If after nine years the board's bylaws failed to shoo me off, I left of my own accord. I know governance, the principles for leading a group. I know the danger when a few people dominate too long.

## CAREER PROBES

In nonprofits, low-cost probes turn on volunteerism. But what if you need entirely different work? How do you probe for a new career?

After five years as a large-firm attorney, and two more as a law professor, Michelle Monse admitted to herself she was bored, and that scared her. What corner had she painted herself into? About that time, a friend told her about Dick Bolles's book, *What Color Is Your Parachute?*

For starters, the book said, she had to identify what didn't bore her. Michelle's interests go wide. She cares about people. Nonprofits and higher education had her attention. With those data points, she cold-called leaders in philanthropies and education to ask for twenty-minute interviews.

"What's a day in the life for you?" she'd ask in person. "What do you love about this work? What don't you like? What credentials got you here?" And the silver bullet: "Is there anyone else you think I should talk to?"

Michelle watched the clock. At the end of twenty minutes, she'd close the interview. In the next twenty-four hours, she'd send a handwritten thank-you note. By the end of eighty conversations (excessive, she admits) with people in varied positions in various nonprofits, she knew what she wanted. She also knew a lot of people in her chosen field.

By the time Michelle started work at a nonprofit, she had taught night law school for interim income and served six months as an unpaid intern for a CEO she met in her first interview. She saw how foundations work, and the foundation saw her. At the end of six months, the CEO said, "We're not about to lose Michelle Monse."

In another decade, Michelle was heading the $90 million King Foundation.

A career probe, in other words, is a series of directed conversations: first with yourself, then with people you might want to be.

## WAS I ALREADY IN GOD'S WORK?

Sixty percent of people who pull off the road to reflect on meaning and work return to their work with new purpose. A much smaller portion will find some hybrid of past skills and future aims. I believe that's my next chapter: using my for-profit knowledge in agriculture and business to help investors help feed the world.

For the better part of three decades I poured myself into one company, and that company was all I knew. For a decade after, I diversified into a portfolio of nonprofits and saw a world of needs.

Now I want to see profitable investments address widespread need. Some like-minded investors and I already have tested the idea in the supply chain, and it works. So far, the investments are best suited in farmland. For the long-term benefit of shareholders and the flourishing of millions, private equity has an exciting future.

## NONPROFIT PURPOSE, FOR-PROFIT MEANS

Enter Triquetra (*tri-ke-tra*), a business model we named for the Celtic infinity knot, a three-strand crux for a triple-impact aim at common good, human flourishing, and financial return.

The Triquetra model can unite, streamline, and grow companies that are doing good. Most often they will be in agriculture or in staples such as water, health, infrastructure, and housing. The Triquetra concept connects life-sustaining businesses to investors eager to advance their services and values. In this model all member companies answer to independent boards, certifications, policy compliance, and financial audits. The endgame is true corporate social responsibility. Once it's fully engaged, God's will and events will direct its course.

You hear my energy. You see I've come from a single company in global ag to many companies using ag to serve the world. Your hybrid route, if you go that way, will be similarly you, similarly unique. What you do will tap what you're made to do. I'll be a mentor—a coach—eager to help and work with people and companies able to run with the idea.

## YOUR CALL AND RESPONSE

Until further notice, or until the unexpected, this is my calling. It didn't come overnight. Few callings do. To begin to get to yours, the route is common sense, counsel, and prayer. You start with yourself, your interests, and active probes. You try ideas and roles on for size. You make informed mistakes and look for surprises. How do you hear God? You listen. You read and seek the counsel of people in the know and people who know you.

Will you ever know for sure? Not by an audible voice. There's a reason it's called faith.

----

The day at the board meeting, as my devotion on meekness ended, chatter died off and the photo of my daughter circled back. I felt certain not of group direction but of shared love and understanding, and of trust in next things. Step by step: not full knowledge but growing confidence.

I said to myself: *This is what it's like at the center of God's work and will.* It's not clarity, but it is faith. Your trust that direction comes.

Life gives us times to wait and times to serve, keeping in mind that a calling today can change tomorrow. As we grow weary or hit diminishing returns, we ask again, listen again, try again, recharge . . . maybe again seek out a new assignment.

*Because God gives us spirits and minds.*

## ASK YOURSELF

1. Is decision-making easy or difficult for me? Why or why not?

2. When I face a big life decision, how do I choose?

3. If God were at work in my life—in a situation, ministry, relationship, or project—how do I think I'd know?

4. How do I define a calling? If I had one, how would I know?

5. If I were to try a new role on for size—anything at all—what interests me?

RESOLVE

# CHAPTER FIVE

# BE INTENTIONAL

*In Writing*

RESOLVE

"A goal without a plan is just a wish."

— **Antoine de Saint-Exupery**

In August 1944, two months after the D-Day invasion, a magazine called *Popular Mechanics* put numbers to the massive logistics that had turned the tide of World War II. From England, the Allies had spirited 156,000 troops a hundred miles across the English Channel to surprise the enemy's coastline defense. Next to the monumental surge of soldiers, ships, and supplies on Normandy's beaches, the writer said, Napoleon's battle plans looked like a game of checkers.

I've stood on the far side of that channel, at Omaha Beach, where Americans soldiers waded ashore. A U.S. Navy memorial there calls it the greatest amphibious incursion in history. No marker salutes the architects of the day, but they factor in every story, every foot of Normandy soil.

"Plans are useless," General Eisenhower often said to his troops. "Planning is everything."

## WHY PLAN

I know about lack of plans.

The day I became a CEO, I inherited a company with no clear path. The CEO before me had adapted the company to industry change. Now the global market had become a raging sea, and we were rudderless. *What do we do now, and how do we do it together?* Across hundreds of employees, multiple sites, and varied operations, no master plan existed to marshal our hundred-plus leaders—a leader defined as anyone supervising anyone else—into a single, unified operating force.

In that vacuum, one of my first acts as CEO was to hire Dr. Jon

Hope of Rockhurst University, a planning-system fanatic and author of an unpublished textbook called *Seizing Opportunity.* Dr. Hope was a teacher who came for a course and stayed for a decade.

Corporate life was a new experience for Dr. H, with his signature gray hair, which we all assumed came in his service in Vietnam. He'd flown 198 missions. He'd trained in Command and Control Systems. War isn't the only crucible of clarity, but Vietnam left him free of ambiguity, and he wanted that for us too. "If our mission is to go take the hill," he'd say in a class, "we need to be that clear."

Next to truth, clarity sets a person free. Or an organization. I know because Dr. Hope came into our corporate Tower of Babel and hit reverse. He made us weight our words with real meaning, starting with the potentially loaded word *trust*, which he made us define together.

Our employees, we learned, defined "trust" in terms of face time—scheduled meetings, one-on-ones with decision-makers, specific dates to hear and be heard. Knowing that, I formed a half-dozen-page document detailing all company gatherings, from board meetings to annual employee sit-downs with frontline supervisors. Besides open-door talks, every employee could expect scheduled monthly access to a superior on any topic. To build trust, we'd have to talk to each other.

Our work to define trust was a toe in the ocean of the words we had to be clear on. Companywide we wrestled down terms like "market channels," "critical success factors," "dynamic objectives," and "business lifecycle stages." Goodbye, jargon. Hello, common values. With our new lexicon and on hard-won common ground, we hammered out a corporate vision statement and, from there, we defined our objectives, strategies, and tactics.

I can't say our company ever reached full harmony, but in the new era of clear words and purpose, across fifteen market segments, you could hear a hum.

Even now, as I tell these stories about Dr. Hope, I shake my head to think that I came up in middle management, first at a national processing company, then at an international food company, and this was my first brush with an integrated plan. It's true that my previous employers had boomed. But, I'd argue, at their workers' expense. By definition, a company system with no clear process is top down, where employees closest to the jobs have the least say. Human resources drain through the cracks, and bad decisions happen.

"You need to trust people," Dr. Hope would say to us, "but most important, you need to trust the process and the system."

## POWER ON THE PAGE

If it's true that a good plan can clarify and unify corporations and lives, it's just as true that most people would rather go to a dentist than create one. "If that's you," I say when I speak to conference audiences, "if you can swear on a spreadsheet you know that ambiguity kills and you still can't put your values, dreams, and priorities on a page, you can either ditch the idea or you can innovate."

About that time in my talk, on a large screen up goes an original vision statement for my son, Jake, the photographer who cannot, cannot put his future in words. In place of a written anything, the screen shows a collage of photos and cutouts, every picture a visual record of Jake's loves and aspirations.

In my twenties I was Jake, leaving my ideas and dreams to roll across the floor of my mind. Eventually, I caught on that mental-floor ideas mostly stay where they are. Or when they fail, it's easy to rationalize. *I was never serious,* I could say. But words or images on paper close escape hatches. You can erase or delete or rewrite, but the revision says, "Lesson learned. Now to correct course."

RESOLVE

## MAKE YOUR PLAN, TAKE YOUR TIME

The first time I tried to write a life plan, I was delusional. "I'm no corporation," I mused. "I'll have it in an hour." And yes, a single life is less involved than a $4 billion company. And true, a personal plan averages three pages compared to a corporation's fifty-page-plus plan. But in a life plan with harmony, as in a work strategy, all steps are interdependent. And they don't write themselves.

Abe Lincoln famously said if he had six hours to fell a tree, he'd spend the first four sharpening his axe. To sharpen a life plan, you may have to walk away and come back. You may have to edit, think, edit, and at various points jot notes. Ideas may come in the shower, the car, and your kids' soccer games. But finally, one day, every heading will have something under it, and you can say to yourself, "Until something changes, this is it."

A hand goes up. *What life plan do you recommend?* I see that hand, and I have no answer except to tell you to look at plans and innovate.

Adapt from what you see that you like. Talk to people who seem to have directed lives. Gather information. When our company needed a plan, we had Dr. Hope, a teacher and coach. (I recommend a coach, either someone you hire or a friend or mentor.) Not everything Dr. Hope taught could be adapted into a personal plan, but it was more than I knew, and it got me started.

My life plan today, which appears below, shows Dr. Hope's influence and that of people I've known, books I've read, conversations, essays, studies, sermons, and daily experience. I innovated, for goodness' sake, as you will. I knew enough to absorb and adapt—to try on ideas and, by all means, to allow for mistakes. And it's still a work in progress. But in fact—and this is your cue—*any plan beats no plan.*

My current plan starts with my vision, values, and mission. Yours will come together your way. By the end of this book, plans in general will make more sense to you. For now read this one for the logic, and see what speaks to you. Circle and underline. When you write your plan, those will be good places to begin.

# LIFE PLAN

## VISION
To make dreams a reality.

## VALUES
His purpose over my preference.

*See God at work. Allow for guidance through ambiguity. Cultivate a quiet heart governed by the Holy Spirit. Lead a life of harmony. Access life beyond control and measure.*

- **CLEAR SIGHT:** Circumstantial signs. Commanding Scripture. Common sense. Compelling Spirit. Counsel of saints.

- **COURAGE:** Be an ethical, honest, gracious, bold, strong, and devoted follower of Jesus. Follow my own heart and intuition.

- **FAITH:** Love the Lord my God with all my heart, soul, and mind. Love my neighbor as myself. Act justly, love mercy, and walk humbly.

- **PERSEVERANCE:** Pursue a long obedience in the same direction with the strength to stand, the willingness to leap, and the wisdom to know the difference.

RESOLVE

## MISSION

Develop an entrepreneurial and innovative business designed to lift thousands of lives through great governance, strategic vision, positive influence, and orchestrated resources for a portfolio of exceptional corporations with common purpose, unity, and trust.

## CRITICAL SUCCESS FACTORS

- **Do the right thing:** Build meaningful relationships with a targeted, small, and diverse portfolio of organizations that are healthy, strong, and receptive. Understand their vision, share their passion;

see the attitude, aptitude, and resources needed to drive the success they desire.

- **The right way:** Invest wisely in the organizations at the right time to release the energy, ideas, passion, and spirit that builds the team.

- **With economy:** Shape a flexible life plan to enjoy deeply and reap the rewards of the relationships across the portfolio, independent of any one group for success.

## OBJECTIVES BY CIRCLE OF LIFE

Relationships and relevance shape a better legacy and life.

**Community life: Live with faith, hope, and love.**

- Follow Jesus as a disciple, investor, leader, and steward.

- Be a life learner in agriculture, community, economics, fitness, religion, and travel.

- Pursue vocational innovation, leadership, and stewardship to finish well together in our next chapters.

**Marketplace life: Create higher standards of living to drive freedom and liberty.**

- Focus on expertise in agriculture, capital, commodity, energy, government, professional, transportation, and vocational stewardship.

- Invest family and foundation capital through a diverse network of professional advisors to give and live from the growth and income.

- Have leading roles in firms in growing markets with high-performing teams and ample resources for success.

**Personal life: Glorify God in all we do.**

- Grow with Debbie in faith as parents, as a family, with friends, as neighbors, in healthy habits, and to fulfill lifetime passions.

- Invest wisely our time, treasure, and talent. Give generously. Earn, save, and give all we can.

- Parent our children to understand the gospel, grow in faith, know their gifts, be great friends, get an education, stay physically fit, and steward their resources.

- Travel for family memories, international point of view, and life-long learning.

**Philanthropy: Help those less fortunate and spread the gospel globally.**

- Connect to people with shared passions to match talent, time, and treasure.

- Develop next-generation leadership.

- Increase results in workplace development with God's culture.

## STRATEGY

The journey ahead requires a roadmap.

Pursue my passion to see people and organizations lead positive change to increase success and make a difference. Select organizations that see big opportunity and face challenging circumstances, and groups wanting to grow but unsure how, seeking expertise. My primary roles are corporate advisor, director, entrepreneur, executive, and investor from decades of experience and success as a company builder, corporate board leader, international business executive, and compassionate capitalist. The platform for corporate activity is Clear Sight (Holdings & Ventures). There is fun in the work and joy in the journey of life. Success is measured in significance and in surrender to God.

## TACTICS
What needs to be done?

- **CONNECT:** Link with businesses, nonprofits, and marketplace trade groups and in philanthropy. Seek decision-makers restless with the status quo, wanting to lead positive change.

- **LEARN:** Study the circumstances and desired results, then entrepreneurially and flexibly craft a way to work together. Determine where to serve based on referrals; receptiveness; strategic value; experience; and the measure of common purpose, unity, and trust.

- **SERVE:** Eyeing both the future and the present, serve together to make sense of the complexity of their situation, to clarify direction, to align resources, to develop structure, and to organize to engage their people to drive the change they desire.

- **LEAD:** Identify simple success in sharp increases in desired results.

# CONTROLS

Set measures.

### Leading Indicators

- Community, family, personal, and work-life integration

- Fun in the work

- High engagement and focus

- Life with family, friends, and neighbors shows the fruit of the Spirit

- Flowing referrals and new opportunities

### Trailing Indicators

- Benefits exceed costs

- Contentment and satisfaction

- Use of God-given gifts

- Joy in the journey

- Growth of influence of personal brand

### My Results Journal

- Regular Sunday review of both qualitative and quantitative results in my *Book of Life*

My father's interest in World War II meant that our family Christmases always brought surprises for his kids and grandkids and predictably had biographies and history books for him. His Marine stint in the Pacific theater, day after day, shift after shift, had been in a vacuum of news from both the European and Pacific fronts. For the rest of his life, the books, I think, were his reach for the big picture.

"Big picture" is business-speak for "why," and the day came when I needed my own big picture. I needed more than a day at the office, or a string of productive days, to have a sense of my place in the cosmos. How routinely we reduce our contributions in life to slots on a spreadsheet. How easily we accept that an act that can't be measured is therefore less important. Metrics are an illusion of control. Faith alone takes us to reality beyond our control.

When faith factors into our work, we still look for results, but we also recognize moments beyond what we can see, much less measure. In those moments, I think, our work flows out of our personal dreams, informed by prayer, inspired by the masters before us. We see God at work and know we're part of it. In those moments, spreadsheets fall away. But to get to those moments, we need our big picture.

My first glimpse of my big picture came at the end of my career with a plan that would take more years to understand: a whiteboard drawing of a cross, a bull's-eye, a dollar sign, and a heart. You don't have to wait that long. As your big picture begins to form—tomorrow, in six months, or next year—I'm convinced it will come through your work on a plan.

Because plans are useless, but planning is everything.

# ASK YOURSELF

1. Am I spontaneous or too committed to routine? What is my history of making and using any kind of plan?

2. Do I have a sense of where I want my life to go? Why or why not?

3. When I make lists, what do they do (or not do) for me? If they fall short, where or when does that happen?

4. When have I set and achieved a goal? At any point was any part of setting that goal in writing? How did that work for me? If not in writing, how do I keep a goal top of mind?

5. What stops me from starting a plan?

RESOLVE

**CHAPTER SIX**

# FOCUS

*Right Work, Right Time*

RESOLVE

"[Character is] built externally by making
commitments to things—to a spouse or family,
to a philosophy or faith, to a community
and to a vocation. And how well we choose
those things and execute those things
determines the fulfillment of our lives."

**— David Brooks**

N ewcomers to western Kansas are struck by the vast sameness. From my parents' place near Holcomb up the fifteen miles to our northern fields, in every direction, for as far as anyone can see, the scene is flat and unchanging. The few breaks are a farmhouse here, a grain elevator there. Even locals can lose their way.

Even this local. My brother, Stan, and I were in our early teens when Dad promoted us to summer and weekend work on the tractors. A section is a mile square, and a day's work might involve several sections. To move from one section to the next, Dad drove the tractor and we'd follow in the pickup with the fuel.

For two teenage boys, the puttering behind Dad's tractor could be mindless torture. At the end of forever, he'd turn in at a new worksite, and we would set up whatever implement was needed.

When at last the day came for me to change fields on my own, instead of a new birth of freedom, what I got was a baptism in low-grade panic. On roads I'd grumbled over, aware of nothing but the tractor in front of me, everything I thought I knew was in the air. *This turn?* I'd ask myself. *This field? Is that the one from yesterday? Did I set the implement right?*

## YES AND NO

Economics is the study of scarce resources in unlimited want, meaning my master's degree in economics was an education in choice. And choice has consequences. To choose any one action is to reject all others. Furthermore, the action you choose will either drain or replenish your resources. Big-scale choices write the world's story.

How we choose for our personal time, resources, and talents writes ours.

That tie between resources and choice was scorched into me my sophomore year at KSU. I'd agreed to help revive an ag econ club, where membership was small and energy low. In truth, the group was redundant, but I said I'd do it. The semester I poured my limited time into a lost cause taught me the law of unreplenished energy, namely that it serves no one. When the club closed, I was back to finding a new field.

Unlike the Kansas landscape, our fields in life overlap: our relationships, our work in the marketplace, our spare time, what we do for others. The field we go to may be global, national, local, or personal, but to take it, to say yes to it, depends just as much on how you say no. And that's a conversation worth having.

Several years ago, the *Journal of Consumer Research* published an eleven-page report called "I Don't vs. I Can't"[1] about, of all things, the word *no*. People who have trouble saying it, to paraphrase the report, waste time in the wrong fields.

Our word choices matter. "I can't" leaves a hole a mile wide for a magazine salesman or volunteer coordinator to drive through. "I don't" says you have a plan, and this isn't on it. Move along.

There's a line in the Broadway show *Pippin* that says, "If I'm never tied to anything, I'll never be free," and those are words to live by. To live by a weak yes, to commit fully to nothing, to hope to forever keep

RESOLVE

---

[1] Vanessa Patrick and Henrik Hagtvedt, "'I Don't' versus 'I Can't': When Empowered Refusal Motivates Goal-Directed Behavior," *Journal of Consumer Research* 39, no. 2 (August 2012): 371–381, https://doi.org/10.1086/663212.

every option, first of all, is naive and, second, is a big no to real life. A firm no can be learned, and for a good life, it must be.

A career counselor responded to the *Journal of Consumer Research* article in the opinion page of the *New York Times*. A go-getter is not the person who says yes to everything, the counselor said. Just the opposite. It's when people learn to say no that careers take off.

## A THOUSAND NOS

At KSU every freshman lives in a dorm, a life-size yes to diversity and fun, and a passive no, in my case, to good grades. It took my sophomore-year move into the FarmHouse fraternity house, where the rules said no for me, to revive my GPA.

We work to master our every yes and no because life balance is a myth. No one can do everything. (Only in teams can everyone do something.) My daughter, Grace, born with jaundice, spent the first week of her life in the hospital. For years after, she'd have to make repeat visits to the oxygen tent. My work–family ratio never balanced on Grace's needs, but our family had harmony because the yes from Debbie, consummate mother, counterweighted my no. I write this, of course, knowing single parents make much harder choices.

As time passed, our kids grew, and our parents aged. Again and again, we learned how a thoughtful no can open doors to a better yes. Our classic story was in 1999. We were living in Kansas City, where I headed the company's largest division. The ag world was changing fast and, unknown to me, I'd been earmarked to be the next CEO, which would move our family to Omaha. But Kansas City was our home now, and in a deep sense. I said no to leading from Omaha, knowing that might kill the offer entirely. But it didn't.

What happened next validates the career counselor's words in the *New York Times*. Saying yes to family raised my stock in the eyes of our company chairman. Bending precedent, he let me lead from Kansas City.

## PUT YOUR YES IN WRITING

To everything there is a season. To every yes, there is a sigmoid curve of birth, life, and death. After a decade as CEO, a day came when I left the company and closed my career—this time with more years behind me than ahead. I needed a new dream, a new yes, and like most people at a crossroads, I had to come up with new choices. From years of decision-making, this is where I knew to reach for a pen and pad, because to map a future you start with the borders.

In a barbell of a book called *These Truths*, an historian named Jill Lepore describes an early effect of putting words on paper. When Christopher Columbus took possession of the island of Haiti on behalf of Spain, Lepore said, besides announcing it, he wrote it down. Believe it or not, that was new.

Speech has more urgency than writing, Lepore writes, but spoken words tend to be forgotten while "writing lasts."[2] Columbus's written claims were on the heels of the new Gutenberg press. The civilized world was discovering that words on pages have their own forms of

---

[2] Jill Lepore, *These Truths* (New York: W. W. Norton & Company, 2018).

⬆

## SUGGESTED READING

Any system beats no system, and this book gives you mine. Here are more ideas, and you know the drill: study the dances and find your steps.

- Peter F. Drucker, *Managing Oneself* (Cambridge, MA: Harvard Business Review Classics, 2008).

- Lloyd Reeb, *Success to Significance* (Grand Rapids, MI: Zondervan, 2004).

- Clayton Smith and Dave Wilson, *At the Crossroads* (Nashville: Abingdon Press, 2016).

power. Along with a sense of permanency, they crystalize our thinking and tighten our focus.

And they talk back to us.

As someone with Type-A tendencies, I learned at work that I could think more clearly just by getting my thoughts in writing. That act forced me to be clear. Fast forward to these days, and, true to my organized self, I organize my portfolio of work in a written chart.

Will I show you the chart? Not this time. This book is intended to be a vitamin and not a prescription. Very generally, down the far-left column of my chart I list the four categories I want to keep in harmony: (1) community, (2) marketplace, (3) personal, (4) philanthropy. Across the top, left to right, are my stages of involvement for each group in each category.

For each area of harmony, I list the "teams" in that category. By team, I mean the organization, company, service, you name it, that helps me achieve my goals. Under fitness is my team of Pilates trainers. The chart has no magic. The magic is the concrete act of having a plan and using it to anchor my balloon as opposed to releasing the balloon into the sky.

George Harrison's "Any Road" has a haunting refrain: "If you don't know where you're going, any road will take you there." Between Anywhere and Somewhere is a plan, and I submit to you that it helps immeasurably to have that plan in writing.

RESOLVE

## REDUCING INDECISION

As a teenager driving farm machinery on my own, after a little hit and miss, I'd eventually find the right field. No harm done. In college, when a single fee covered a set number of courses, I'd overenroll and try everything. In those years for the first two weeks, at least, of any semester, I'd walk into classrooms wondering if I was in the right one.

The business world ends the grace period for indecision. As market sectors barrel at high and sustainable rates, you either act now or repent later. When it works, you're euphoric. But all-out commitments on limited information can also hit walls and splat—teaching me, as much as I could, to anticipate. To think through an action or choice in writing, results in fewer walls, fewer splats.

Preparation is everything. The reliable thirty-years-and-a-goldwatch careers went out with the rotary phone. Twentysomethings today know the single constant is no constants. A stint at a megacorporation like Microsoft or Google is to springboard to something smaller. The point is to be ready. Plans will change with opportunity and chance, but never doubt that plans matter.

If you're in your twenties or thirties and uncertain about your career, find your yes and master your no. Get your thoughts on paper, and use the clarity to test and adapt. See how those pages talk back to you. If you're in midlife or retirement age and searching for a new field, the clarity of plans on a page never mattered more.

## ASK YOURSELF

1. How do I know when work is right for me?

2. How well do I say no or draw lines? How does that affect what I can say yes to?

3. What do I want from life?

4. When does my life feel passive, like guessing, or like steps in the dark? Would definable goals make a difference?

5. In my life, what would readiness look like?

SECTION 3

# RESPOND

# CHAPTER SEVEN

# GO TOGETHER

*The Outsized Power of Shared Purpose*

RESPOND

"True freedom is not the absence of constraints
but rather the choice of liberating constraints.
We are always bound to something."

**— Tim Keller**

S hortly after I was made CEO of a privately held business, the family representative and I attended a workshop together at Northwestern University in Evanston, Illinois. Companies like ours tend to be laws unto themselves. We needed to know our legal options and set our guidelines. In the workshop, we were surrounded by cases in point. For instance, several of our classmates were from a sixth-generation firm in Belgium with longstanding, steel-edged rules. Just to get in, a family member had to build and succeed at a separate business. By age fifty-five, that place on the management team would close shut. We're talking family-business survival of the fittest.

Why such harsh guidelines? To save lives, I say only half-jokingly. In a public firm, an unhappy investor can sell and walk. In a private firm, siblings and other directors may lob grenades across a board table and unity may blur into a Rorschach blot, but no one goes anywhere. The only recourse is the rules.

Our instructor at the workshop, John L. Ward, was a world expert in contractual family dynamics. The groups that survive and thrive, he told us, forge alignment in common purpose, unity, and trust. One, two, three. In my notes I scribbled the words, circled them, and added "team."

Life works in teams, I believe, because my own life has unrolled as a series of every possible order of group, organization, club, service, business, partnership, friendship, or agency—ad hoc and long term. If you have a pulse, teams have advanced your life. Yes, it's possible for an individual team to devolve into groupthink or disunity. More often, though, a group of people with a common goal do what no single person ever can.

I think I've always known teams do more than compete. When my high school sports career ended, FarmHouse fraternity narrowed my focus and opened my world. In my early career, in every new city, professional and local organizations were also social onramps. My church's small groups informed my business education; my marriage and family continue to teach and reteach me the fundamentals of team dynamics. Near the end of my career, I knew enough about teams to help pioneer what became the Commodity Market Council, a merger of industry rivals whose all-star unity made each one stronger in the world market.

The opposite of team is independence, which Americans esteem to a fault and columnist David Brooks calls the national lie. How many times have I seen "freedom" become its own trap, when it's our commitments, what Brooks calls "the chains we choose," that set us free?

They set us free even as they unite us. This chapter is about the outsized power of shared purpose.

## THE STRONGER *ME* IN *WE*

RESPOND

In 1992, I was a relatively new corporate officer and by now a keen student of teams. This was during the period after my father's death, when Debbie and I joined what turned out to be a booming church. As I described earlier, we saw a funeral-home congregation of two hundred explode to what would be twenty-two thousand people on five campuses. But there's more. As the church moved from the margins to mega, I saw a churchwide surge occur not top down, but from the inside out—through a widening network of small groups of eight to fifteen people each. And every group outperformed the sum of its parts.

Sunday mornings, as Debbie and I sat in the pew watching video updates, we saw church volunteers—men and women very likely bored at their day jobs—outshine and outperform professionals in the same work, floors above their pay grades. I'm thinking of Habitat for Humanity; Matthew's Ministry for special-needs kids; and outreaches to prisoners, foster kids, addicts, and more. I'd watch the videos and think, *Do these people's managers at work know the talent they're sitting on?*

One Sunday I resolved never again to overlook the obvious. That Monday at work, I began to form teams. Forget income, background, education, or title. Forget ties, heels, and collars. Nobody was nobody. And we proceeded to see at work, as I saw at church, that to the degree a job had the right people, *whoever they were*, the better the me rose to we, and the higher the output.

Managers run hot and cold on teams—how to use them, whether to embrace them, what they mean—but progress runs on cooperation, and that's a whole book in itself. We humans are wired to achieve together.

Maybe as you read that you're mentally trolling for exceptions. Al-

> ⊕
>
> "The more you invest in the bettering of other lives, the more you participate in human flourishing for a greater number of people, the richer relationally your own life becomes. You won't learn that until you do it. If you focus only on relationships that fuel your aspirations for your life, then the smaller your world grows, the less rich relationally your life will be. The more you understand the least of these, the more you will see yourself and God."
>
> —Ray Carter,
> Chicago Men's Fellowship

bert Einstein, you think. There's a loner who recast the universe for us. But E=MC² didn't come to a man in a vacuum. Einstein in Munich didn't make his own meals or teach himself mathematics. Sometime google Helen Dukas, Einstein's secretary, housemate, and protector of the great man's time, privacy, reputation, and eventually his legacy. She may be a footnote to a footnote, but her employer's work for the ages turned on the hours and space she helped create and enforce.

We all have people who got us further down the road. Parents, school nurses, friends, bosses, camp counselors. From my first steps across the living room floor to high school track competitions; from 4-H livestock judging to global supply chain; from walking into a makeshift church to a walk with God, if I've passed a milestone or brushed a goal, what I know that Albert Einstein knew is that nothing significant, personal or public, ever happens alone.

## STARTING OVER? FIND A TEAM

Why does a soldier re-up in wartime? Not to take lives but to get back to life, says war journalist Sebastian Junger. In *Why Veterans Miss War*, Junger says soldiers return to battle for the community and identity missing at home. I get how crisis puts us all in the same foxhole. Bullets fly, and suddenly it's about more than me. We saw it in the COVID-19 pandemic. We see it after hurricanes and floods and earthquakes. But one day the crisis ends, the urgency winds down, and with the intensity goes the joy of common purpose. We're back to demands for what I want, now.

And we're the lesser for it. Soldiers know that the fixed center of

RESPOND

gravity is a "we" and that to have it for any length of time is to suffer when it's gone. I saw my father's nostalgia for his war years, for the high-stakes solidarity. Something like that shows up in athletes who long for the camaraderie of high school or college teams. I see it in former employees who, for whatever reason, find themselves out of work with no plan.

If you know that feeling, I can tell you, as I long to tell any one of them, that every ending carries the seeds of a new beginning. *You can find it.* When you graduate or your kids do, when you leave a job or it leaves you, when you survive a health scare or someone you love falls to one, when you move or land on a significant birthday . . . there's more ahead than Netflix and a couch. You can absorb the hurt and catch your breath. You search for a partner, a team, or a reason to form one. You experiment, risk, allow for mistakes, look for the unexpected. And when any part of what you do hits a wall and the wall doesn't give, you try something else.

My friend Drew Hiss built a company called the Acumen Group, a peer-learning network for leaders. A couple of years ago, through the Group, I tried to form a "sage" team of former execs and business owners to pursue new beginnings together. The concept called for at least a dozen members, but it never drew more than five or six, and after half a year we closed. A few months ago over coffee Drew and I bemoaned having no team in the journey to finish well. But in God's economy, no effort is wasted. In some form, we'll salvage what we learned and use it.

# THE TEST OF SUCCESS

In the mid-1980s, when the US government left the grain business, like a fish on dry land my company had to flop from storage in silos to just-in-time shipping. And because our governance model discouraged equity investors, we had to both quickly liquidate and quickly invest.

To do that, our CEO, Butch Fischer, split the company into two divisions: one to divest us of past assets, and one to promote current assets and build new ones. I headed the second, and like a SWAT team on new terrain, for every group in our division, we set best practices, built plans, and snapped into new financial structures. The teamwork was addictive. The work eventually succeeded, and a day came when we stood back in awe.

And then I learned two things: First, I learned that true success outstrips the sum of the people involved. The results dwarfed us all. Second, I learned that it takes problems—tragedies, even—for people to move in unison. Only in a crisis will so many so willingly try new steps, embrace radical improvements, risk failure. To be sure, the panic to rebuild our company in the midst of industry flux was like a seven-year ride on the Sky Screamer at Six Flags. But after a string of cliff climbs and drops, we caught our breath, and we flew.

RESPOND

After I became a CEO, I got a lesson in the problems of prosperity, when challenges wane and *us* dulls back to *me*. Pettiness rears its horned head, and cracks in company alignment can become canyons. Crises can forge bonds, and success can breed selfishness.

# MY TEAM LESSONS FOR LIFE

When I became a CEO, I went from leading a single team—my oper-ating division—to leading the entire company, an international team of one hundred frontline managers, each one over a team of five or six people. Until then, half of our workforce had worked independently; now everyone, *everyone*, had to upgrade to "we." Haltingly to start, eventually with flow, we built and blended our in-house groups, fold-ing in new competencies from the outside. Our days flowed into var-ied series of changes, trials, mistakes, and hard-won successes. From that era so rich in lessons of human dynamics, to put it mildly, a list of boots-on-the-ground truths stay with me and may be helpful for you.

Helpful how? In giving you the sweat-soaked encouragement to ride the waves, share the grunting before you claim the glory, take the long view, be a servant, and make friends. Don't be deceived by the simplicity of what you read here. From a man of lists, I can tell you this one is gold.

This also is the first time I've ever put all this together.


- **Favoritism can be fatal.** A strong team gives energy, but to throw all your energy into any one team will most likely backfire. (This is why investors build portfolios.) Monthly, still, as I survey my chart of current groups, I ask: *In their context, how are they doing? Where can I help the greater good?* What I don't ask is: *Which group do I like best, and how can I emphasize it to the exclusion of the others?*

- **Aptitude can't be forced.** Where a team is weak—and every team has weaknesses—for heaven's sake, import talent. To force an existing employee or group to manufacture the skills missing, at *best*, will get you average results.

- **In a tough market, less is more.** In difficult times, seek equilibrium and forget the big win. Work with what's working and, like a farmer, practice patience. Some years, some days, your highest goal is to limit the loss.

- **Success is for sharing.** In our company's mental move from me to we, profit sharing profited us all. Even our smaller, more independent in-house groups gained by their own performances, by the successes of groups around them, and from overall company progress. *E pluribus unum.*

- **Stay current.** Big change turns on conversations big and small—and ongoing. Besides our annual town hall meeting series, I traveled to major offices to visit with all manner of large groups. Frequent conference calls fortified our mid-year leadership meetings and frontline manager talks. We never had magic; we only had ears.

- **Use business to make friends.** The second-oldest profession is grain trade, and I've seen international grain deals safely go where governments feared to tread. I've seen trade relationships open breathing space and time for official relations to catch up. As often as possible, use your business to open new ground for common good.

- **Troughs happen.** Hard times are a fact, and it's the businesses that resist cycles that become roadkill. The ones that survive use the inevitable troughs to hit reset. They adjust expectations, find ways to improve, and come out stronger for it.

RESPOND

- **Love thy nonleaders.** "Cogs" are essential workers who deserve full respect. Most companies give their workers accountability, but for employees to think independently *and* take group ownership, everyone—including the "cogs"—should have authority, resources, and a vision of the big picture.

- **Safety leads to risk and vice versa.** In the words of Seth Barnes, World Race teambuilder, an effective group offers the safety to risk and then unites *because* of risk. Where one group member is vulnerable and another reciprocates, trust can take root.

- **Good leaders are good followers.** The shining lesson of the Commodities Market Council, a story I return to often, is that true leaders do whatever is needed and, as needed, help other leaders lead.

## WHEN CHOOSING TEAMS

Now to roll up our sleeves. The teams you may need to join, or form, will flow from your plan of action. The teams in my life flow out of my four areas of harmony: my community, the marketplace, my personal life, and philanthropy.

In each area, to find "my teams," I talk to friends and read newspapers, magazines, and websites (like CEOExpress.com). I survey and study all active groups, companies, and organizations. When one catches my eye, I have a two-part filter.

1. **I build only on islands of health and strength.** Especially in nonprofits, a good cause can blind us to bad management. Instead of trying to prop up a dysfunctional team or organization, find what

is working and fan it. Also, before you build your own company or organization, consider that a startup has a 10 percent likelihood for success; a franchise has a 75 percent chance.

2. **I work only with the receptive, only with what's trying to happen.** In groups or one on one, never force a relationship or an idea. If you're having to sell yourself or your dream, that tells you to press the brakes and pull over. You want to proceed only on shared vision.

## YOU ALONE CAN DO IT, BUT YOU DON'T HAVE TO DO IT ALONE

Once on a family trip to Africa, Jake photographed a single-horned antelope separated from the herd and left for lion bait. It was painful to witness, and my comment now is to not do that to yourself. Independence gets you to a point, then abandons you. To go far, go with others.

In the work to build that global force known as the Commodity Markets Council, our colossal challenge was to consolidate groups from divergent commodities—from grains, meats, base metals, precious metals, energy—into a single trade group. On their own, like that antelope, they were easy prey.

Individually, the commodities groups in the council were each other's competitors. At the same time, because they functioned similarly, they could benefit from economy of scale. They could share a staff, for instance. As individual and narrow "rights" (or fears) gave way to collective moves, each group gained the individual power to do more than ever.

RESPOND

Teams are so many things. My first was my parents and siblings. My last will be my wife and kids. Between are friendships and groups—large, small, formal, informal, professional, volunteer, simple, and complex—that lift me and help me lift others.

Know yourself, find the groups that share your vision, and advance your dream. It's that basic. You still have to manage within a team, and that's another box of skills. If you have goals, or think you could use some, look around for teams.

## ASK YOURSELF

1. What is my strongest memory or impression regarding a team, any team?

2. How do I define a good team? What does it do and not do?

3. What groups or organizations matter to me? What does it mean to me to belong to it? (Or why do I wish to?)

4. Where am I potentially trying to force something that is not happening?

5. If a team is defined as two or more people with a shared objective, what are my objectives, and what teams could help me advance them?

# CHAPTER EIGHT

# BE BOLD

*Do Things That Take Your Breath Away*

RESPOND

"Therein lies the nobility of our faith, that
we have the heart to dare something."

**— Saint John Henry Newman**

I was in eighth grade when Dad moved us into a house closer to town and began making updates on our old farmhouse, a three-bedroom prairie throwback to army housing.

A thirteen-year-old gives little thought to where money comes from. But when the summer wheat crop got hailed that year, I heard Mom say, "We'll have to put the rest of the house on hold." Dad had a different conclusion, and what he came to was my first course in risk.

Make that calculated risk. Dad had a summer and a fall crop. He had winter income from working cattle. Our wheat had a little crop insurance, and Mom taught school. So our income was diversified. Looking back with a degree in economics, none of my high-level risk–reward decisions have ever improved on the gamble that Dad hedged that summer because, in fact, *gamble* is the wrong word.

In college one day, in Professor Schruben's class on grain marketing, we learned the difference between gambling and a business risk. A racetrack creates risk out of thin air, Professor Schruben said. The winner doesn't matter. To harvest a crop to become food, or to drill oil to convert to fuel, does matter. So while production may seem like a gamble, it will have ways to manage the risk.

I said that the theories I learned in my economics major seldom improved on Dad's common sense, but that didn't stop me from being a know-it-all on occasion. Once, while studying internal rates of return at school, I advised Dad on how to apply the principles to his projects. He let me talk, and then he went on intuitively making decisions good for his overall business. His operating theory was, "Make it work, and it'll make things better."

Now I get it.

## BOLDNESS IS A MENTAL POSTURE

Most of my regrets now, in life and work, are for the risks I didn't take. Not every time, not risk for its own sake, but when my intuition said to go and my head or heart held me back. I shouldn't have feared it because failure also teaches. My regrets now are for my failures to try.

The mental posture to risk is boldness, a state of mind in continuous improvement because it builds on experience. It grows as we grow. And it's both rational and humble. People who misapply boldness can be brash, defiant, even foolish. But true boldness turns on judgment and faith, not vanity.

Remember the final-exam questions: "What did you do about Jesus? And what did you do with the gifts I gave you?" The first time I heard them, my answer to the first question was warm, almost passive. *I embrace what Jesus did*, I thought. *I rest on it.* The second question echoes the parable of the off-site master. As I recall, it caused some shifting in seats. Matthew and Luke both repeat Jesus's story of the landowner who leaves three of his servants to oversee portions of his assets. When he returns, two of the servants have invested and hand him the profits. The third, with the smallest amount, buried his portion and sat on it. Nothing lost, nothing gained.

The first two servants knew their master's mind. "Well done," their master says to them. "You've been faithful with a few things. I'll put you in charge of many." The third servant rejects trust out of hand. "You're a harsh man," he says, "reaping where you didn't sow and gathering where you didn't scatter seed, so I was afraid. Here, take back what is yours."

RESPOND

The servant who invested in fear reaps loss. "For the one who has will be given more," Jesus says, "and he will have more than enough. But the one who does not have, even what he has will be taken from him."

Of course, "What did you do with what I gave you?" assumes we *know* what gifts we have. If you're unsure of yours, Clifton-Strengths 34 (formerly StrengthsFinder) has an online exam that takes maybe forty-five minutes, and I recommend it. I urge you also to talk to your friends, parents, spouse, and coworkers. Ask them what you do well and what tasks you would do well to hand off. In general, what do other people reflect back to you? Where your strengths run thin, your partners and team members can fill the gaps. That's what teams do. In J. R. R. Tolkien terms, that's fellowship for the adventure

One more thing, and for this have your pen out: If you feel short on boldness, your hesitation probably says far less about cowardice than about smoldering discontent. A woman or man in the right work typically is a force. If you have to ask, "Is this work that I care about? Are these my priorities or someone else's? Am I good at this? Is this the right team or project?" very likely the answers are no.

## BOLDNESS COMES IN STEPS

Anne Lamott's classic book on writing, *Bird by Bird*, gets its title from her younger brother's fourth grade school assignment. For months he knew when it was due. But in a salute to ten-year-old boys everywhere, he waited until the night before to start. Moved by his son's panic, Anne's dad, a writer, put an arm around his shoulders and said,

"Bird by bird, buddy. Just take it bird by bird." For writing or life, Anne said, that's still the best advice she's ever heard.

My version of bird by bird began when I was eight or nine years old at 4-H fairs showing farm animals—beef cattle, market hogs, sheep. A small calf is about 500 pounds at the time of purchase. By county fair time at summer's end, it could weigh more than half a ton. To get to the show ring, I had to learn to tame my animal to halter and lead. I had to brush his hair coat and clip the long hairs on his face, tail, and underbelly. I had to strap him on his side to a big table, rotate it 90 degrees, and, avoiding kicks, trim his feet to walk properly.

My first face-off with a tabled behemoth left me breathless. But somewhere between early 4-H and my early teens, adults were gone and once-insurmountable animal prep had become routine.

Bird by bird. In his sleep, my father could spin off ways for his kids to have to struggle, master the steps, and move up to the next thing. On a Monday he'd shout instructions up to me on the tractor. Tuesday, I was alone. By the end of the week, I was teaching someone else.

If I had to say how a person overcomes fear and even learns to like it, it helps to be in the right work, as I said earlier. And it happens in steps. Every challenge, every business venture, cold call, contest, presentation, loss, risk, move, or illness breaks into steps, into next things. No one I know conquers a project or defeats a fear overnight, but anyone can do the next thing.

RESPOND

I've seen it work when a friend or family member battles an illness. Between the time a doctor says, "Something's not right" and a formal diagnosis, the patient (and all the loved ones) agonize in the unknown. With a diagnosis comes a way to plan, a reason to

## REGISTER FOR HERO STATUS

In 1987 a FarmHouse alum founded what is now Be the Match: The National Bone Marrow Donor Registry, a bank of currently 11 million marrow profiles. The United States has 330 million people. Given that each marrow match is highly complex, we can beat 4 percent registration. Your candidacy to register ends at age sixty, and the sooner you sign the longer you can serve.

After I registered, by the way, when a need actually arose for my match and I gave, few things in my life have ever felt so good.

shift focus to decisions and steps. Joe Burch, an engineer and former military officer, underwent a harrowing bone-marrow transplant. He couldn't heal overnight, but he could create a spreadsheet to monitor his meds, his therapies, and his body's reactions and their times of day. Yes, it gave him something to control, but the control was more than illusion. It was good information. At his medical appointments, Joe's doctor could survey his laptop screen and quickly modify treatments.

How does boldness play out? Differently for every one of us. A business maxim says to go big or go home. Mother Teresa said the smallest gesture in Jesus's name has eternal value. Mother Teresa's small things took her to war zones and world leaders. Big ideas may launch business-based solutions scaled to human need. However you come at it, if you're open, risk finds you, and in steps, in dailiness, you find your response.

Finally, if anxiety precedes growth, and I submit that it does, I invite you to learn not to fear your fear. You know the saying, "If you can't do it without being scared, then do it scared." Courage, like most virtues, is a muscle. You can begin today to build it.

In my life in rural Kansas, at college, at work, and in my family, certain situations would incite panic in me, forcing me to create steps to manage it. Eventually, I learned to recognize the grip in my gut as adrenaline and to use it, even welcome it. You can too.

## BOLDNESS RESPONDS TO RULES

I say I welcomed the adrenaline. Once, when an airline pilot was asked to name his most exciting flight, he said, "My job is to make sure flights stay unexciting." So, while I advocate boldness and can recognize fear as adrenaline, excitement is never the goal. Progress is, and progress resists one-size-fits-all. When we boldly took our company from regional to global, in a vast frontier of unfamiliar choices, we learned we could reduce the unwanted thrills with a strategy of rules.

That term, "strategy of rules," is from a *Harvard Business Review (HBR)* article, "Strategy as Simple Rules,"[3] that said when choices abound, the best strategy is to choose well. My job was to set the guidelines for how to choose. It was so effective that when I traded leadership of an international company for a portfolio of international nonprofits, again facing a night sky of new choices, I set up a similar strategy.

Whom do you marry? What city do you live in? What work do you pursue? What sports should your child join? How do you choose between two good schools? When your decision has options, how do

RESPOND

---

[3] Kathleen Eisenhardt and Donald Sull, "Strategy as Simple Rules," *Harvard Business Review*, January 2001, https://hbr.org/2001/01/strategy-as-simple-rules.

you narrow the guesses and improve your odds? Answer: first you put in writing, *for* you, what features and qualities need to line up.

When I decided to join various missions (plural), to choose what missions I'd serve, I set up my choices this way.

*The organization will have*

- a global vision to benefit both global and local markets;

- an entrepreneurial culture of aligned interests, shared gains, and a team of teams; and

- an open-capital structure to ensure effective governance, legacy assets, perpetual capital, and a triple bottom line (financial return, common good, and human flourishing) . . .

## TO BOLDLY GIVE

Cochairing our church's capital campaign forced Debbie and me to think through why and how we give. From a longer talk I was asked to give at our church, these remarks turn on the idea that a bold life involves giving.

- Individually and as a family we wrote down our attitudes and beliefs about giving.

- With our collective values in mind, we resolved to earn, save, and give all we could. Meanwhile, in circumstances, cycles, seasons, and stages, God continued to inform and mature our understanding.

- Giving begets giving as well as joy. Internally and tangibly, we grow and learn to steward the resources God gives us.

- A living comes from what we make; a life comes from what we give. The Linvilles try now to live simply, give generously, and build treasure in heaven. Burial pants have no pockets. We pray for God's will in our lives—nothing more, nothing less.

*So I can*

- use my skills, which my original StrengthsFinder test listed as "commanding, futuristic, strategic, self-assurance, and maximizing";

- improve governance, strategic vision, positive influence, and use of resources and talent; and

- reduce complexity, clarify direction, and help increase results.

*The projects will have*

- critical success factors,

- mission-capability requirements,

- resources and risks, and

- term and exit conditions . . .

*So they can*

- bring others to the gospel, help those less fortunate, and

- generate strategic value and return.

RESPOND

Note that this filter in no way guarantees success. What it does is reduce bad guessing. Good rules inform risk, but it's still a risk, and that's good.

## BOLDNESS COMES IN THE RIGHT QUESTIONS

Once in an organization or group, how do you budget your limited time and resources? My guidelines here came in a 1988 *HBR* piece called "Meetings That Work."[4] The writer gave four simple questions that I've never stopped using:

1. What is the plan?

2. What is the rationale?

3. What are the goals?

4. How much?

As I say often, don't underestimate simplicity. To write short answers to short, strong questions is to have to understand the question and to say what you mean. Again, the operative word is short. Brief, concise, succinct. And brief is seldom easy.

A legal-writing expert tells attorneys until they can state their case in seventy-five words or fewer, they don't know it. They'll hide behind foggy words more commonly known as legal jargon. Clear terms and precise phrases may take hours or even days to get to, but until you have them, you're in a cloud. Mark Twain supposedly wrote to someone that if he'd had more time, he'd have written a shorter letter. If brevity challenged the venerable Mr. Twain, and if it can help win cases, then the work to get to brevity is (a) human, and (b) worth the trouble.

Plan, rationale, goals, cost, that's the clarity for which the four questions call. For decades I taught those four filters to hundreds of people whose decisions affected thousands of projects. The questions, and the work to answer them briefly, helped me plan this book and before

---

[4] Paul Lovett, "Meetings That Work: Plans Bosses Can Approve," *Harvard Business Review,* November 1988, https://hbr.org/1988/11/meetings-that-work-plans-bosses-can-approve.

that helped me draft a $100 million acquisition. My batting average with those questions hovers at 1.000 because a project shutdown to prevent a bad outcome is also a win.

Why not test that four-question filter on your next big decision?

If you're still with me, the journey to boldness comes in steps, in sound rules, and in the right questions. Finally, it comes in commitment.

## BOLDNESS COMES IN COMMITMENT

In the early 1980s I entered the ag market just as the US government was ending costly storage programs that had made it the granary to the world. In the next ten years, because of the Freedom to Farm Act, farmers once far down the food chain could bypass government programs and directly access world consumers. *Boom.* Like that, the ag industry was upside down and innovation hit high gear.

As a young trader at Pillsbury, in that new frontier, I saw flour mill operators convert a waste called mill feed into livestock feed. Third-party merchandising (no facilities to own) made it another new business line. From it, more companies formed and grew.

By the time I was a head of a company, a whole string of once-revolutionary new ideas had become business as usual. My company, when I joined, had been Nebraska-centric, concentrated in grain storage. I saw my company explode to more than seventy-five North America bases and the international markets they served, seeds of future foreign–domestic operations, complex, diverse, built to weather the inconstant world market.

RESPOND

In less than a decade, ideas that began as frightening gambles were old hat. What an education in risk: today's cliff is tomorrow's flatland. In terms of personal life, the message is to embrace boldness. *Just start today.* So important, so fundamental is this truth that if it came with a fight song, I'd break out singing now.

> *Whatever you do or dream you can, begin it.*
> *Boldness has genius, power and magic in it!*

Those lines are from a mountain climber named W. H. Murray, who, for his part, was borrowing from Goethe. What invigorates risk with real power, Murray wrote in his book, *The Scottish Himalayan Expedition*, is the decision to start: the commitment.

> *Until one is committed, there is hesitancy, the chance to draw back, always ineffectiveness. Concerning all acts of initiative (and creation), there is one elementary truth, the ignorance of which kills countless ideas and splendid plans: that the moment one definitely commits oneself, then Providence moves too. All sorts of things occur to help one that would never otherwise have occurred. A whole stream of events issues from the decision, raising in one's favour all manner of unforeseen incidents and meetings and material assistance, which no man could have dreamt would have come his way. I learned a deep respect for one of Goethe's couplets: Whatever you can do or dream you can, begin it. Boldness has genius, power and magic in it!* [5]

---

[5] W. H. Murray, *The Scottish Himalayan Expedition* (London: J. M. Dent, 1951).

No decision is a decision, and typically a wrong one. Whoever said, "If it ain't broke, fix it anyway" knew something about progress, because with the smallest thought, almost any idea can be improved.

Boldness is a mentality we can build or rebuild. When a decision overwhelms us, we break it into steps and work the steps. While risk can be thrilling, thrills are not the point. We can set up guardrails, questions, and criteria to avoid unwanted excitement. Finally, we can come to embrace our fears. The power of boldness typically starts *after* we begin, after we commit to whatever comes.

The unknown can be scary, but to park ourselves or our gifts only in what is known is scarier. Risk is an act of love; and boldness is possible because all challenge is really a series of steps, not reckless reactions, but acts with rules and forethought.

And the moment we commit, as Murray said, providence moves too.

## ASK YOURSELF

RESPOND

1. In general, what does risk mean to me? Growing up, and in my family, what did I learn about risk?

2. What do I want that involves risk? What's at stake? If I were to break the risk into steps, what would they be?

3. What's a risk I'm glad I took?

4. If I were to encourage someone to live more boldly, what would I say? Might those words apply to me too?

5. When have I learned to do things in steps, and how did it work for me?

# CHAPTER NINE

# MASTER THE DAILY

*Readiness Is in the Everyday*

RESPOND

"Chance favors the prepared mind."

**— Louis Pasteur**

Dean Erwin was a big man in a small school. At six-foot-six and just out of college ball, he coached basketball—almost taking the Holcomb High School team to state one year—and taught human physiology. While physiology is a worthy course, what Coach Erwin added to our young lives had less to do with sports and academics than readiness.

In the late '60s and early '70s, when hair length was a statement and "clean cut" could be suspect, Coach Irwin wore a tie. His shoes were shined; his hair was military length. On the basketball court he drilled us from the socks up. In class we turned in our notes as part of our grade. Most of us had mastered only appearing to listen. Now we had to critically hear and prioritize information under headings and subheadings.

And what happened was that I learned to hear, write, and recall. Every day we'd work our notebooks, and every day, unaware of our progress, we increasingly were ready for the exam. Do that for a semester, then for a year, and something changes. You realize preparation is readiness, and that readiness attracts opportunity.

Coaches tell their players to know what they can control and what they can't. We can control attitude, prep, and effort. Attitude and effort are states of mind. Preparation is an act. Early in my career as a trader, I had to perform at a consistently high pitch. It never let up. I had to stay ready.

Ready for what? For the expected and the unexpected. Say an athlete has a non-sport-related injury, but she's fit, she's ready, and she heals quickly. Say a businessman hears from a rival's attorney. Turns out the businessman's records are complete and up to date.

He's ready. Say an immigrant teenager new to the United States has no friends, so he spends his summer reading physics books. When his new school starts up, he's ready. My mother, the competent multi-tasker and community leader, kept our home organized too. She never feared drop-ins.

The readiness message in this chapter is routine to me because I've internalized and practiced it for so long. And that's the point. The disciplines we practice in our years of obscurity, when the critical few moments come, have made us ready. Readiness also has something to do with peace, also because lack of preparation can cause great anxiety.

## MASTER THE EVERYDAY

Growing up on a farm, and through high school, the order in my life was external. It came from people and systems around me. Not until college, with all its moving pieces, and with adults no longer making my life their business, did I buy my own date book and begin my own lists. Most people stop there, with dates and lists, in a more or less *Groundhog Day*–type march through their days. And routine is good. But routines are launch sites, not landings. As new tasks, skills, or responsibilities become ordinary, even mindless, our game ratchets up. We add new challenges, scaling again how we master the trivial many to serve the critical few.

As you read this, you may be mentally scanning your own routines. Maybe you rise early to run or have a regular quiet time. You may work out, refer to a reading list, keep a date night, manage a family budget, stay in touch with an elderly parent, water flowers, or main-

RESPOND

tain a journal. Whatever it is, you know the results come with time. Often enough, they come with opportunity.

Did I say readiness was easy? I live in the future, hardwired for strategy. I'd rather think than do, and I resent repetition. But the sublime builds on the mundane. Regular meetings keep us current. Daily workouts secure energy and clarity. Reading adds to knowledge. Classes expose us to new people and ideas, and open networks. Journals, as I go into later, talk back to us.

My routines mix big and small. Mondays through Thursdays I deal with my "critical few" leadership roles, all flowing from my many priorities and teams. Late every week I "sharpen the saw" (as in Lincoln's sharpening for six hours to cut for two), as we all do, with haircuts and dentist appointments, shopping, meetings, and errands. Those are a form of readiness. Eighty percent of our productivity turns on our 20 percent of basics: rest, family, prayer, finances, learning, exercise, diet. Every one is expendable, we think, until a crisis from its neglect shuts down everything else.

## HONOR THE MUNDANE

Brother Lawrence, a seventeenth-century monk, has taught people in every generation since to honor the mundane. God regards not the greatness of the work, he wrote to a close friend, "but the love with which it is performed."

You might underline that line about love. Lawrence was a wounded soldier who found work at a monastery, expecting to give up every pleasure of life. Instead, in the monotony of kitchen duty, which he initially despised, he met the eternal. Not quickly but surely, his tables, floors, bowls, and plates became sacred ground. And a kitchen laborer known to few people at the time, centuries later, is a revered touchstone.

After he died, Brother Lawrence's letters and memories were gathered into a small book titled *The Practice of the Presence of God*, a journal of his learning to do for Jesus, with joy, what he'd long done grudgingly for himself. In his telling, he defines readiness: "I do what I can," he wrote, "and then let him do with me whatever he wants."

As someone with Type-A tendencies, I long considered spiritual disciplines, prayer included, to be arbitrary, even inefficient. Then one day a speaker named James Bryant referred in passing to the disciplines as spiritual training. *Training*, I mused: *if the disciplines are training, then I train and trust God to use it.*

My unending lesson now is that any task done in God's name can lift my line of sight. One day as part of our financial management, Debbie and I bought life insurance from a family friend who came to the house to talk numbers. At some point, looking up from the papers, he asked Debbie if that seemed to be the right amount of coverage on me. Raising an eyebrow, my wife said, "That's a lot of money to take out the trash."

We all laughed. And I like to think I'm more than a daily chore. But in God's economy, every chore is more than a chore, and that's the open secret.

If faith isn't a verb, it's an action noun, a long obedience in the same direction. By faith we daily prepare, per Brother Lawrence, for "whatever he wants"—for the unknown wrapped in a promise we can

RESPOND

trust. In the context of this book, in faith we can become students of ourselves, our proclivities, our gifts. We can make lists and search out answers. We find teams and community, pray and write, pursue wisdom, and come to a singular mission. And much of it is mundane.

But Brother Lawrence is telling us there is no such thing as mundane. In our homework, showers, laundry, taxes, yard work—in even the dreaded Mondays of life—as we cultivate awareness of him, God can surprise us with some sense of himself. Maybe it's as we read or hear something, or maybe a friend calls. Some fear dissolves, or an idea comes to us. Our smallest movement toward God, a breath of a prayer, can open us to more of his everlasting love. In a beige day, when we couldn't possibly gin it up for ourselves, some hope appears, and we glimpse rich hues. We floss our teeth, stand in checkout lines, drop off dry cleaning, and he is there, using everything.

And seen or unseen, through the daily threads the sublime.

## MASTERFUL LISTS

A few years ago in an NPR interview, Dr. Atul Gawande,[6] a surgeon at Brigham Women's Hospital and professor of surgery at Harvard Medical School, talked about the life-saving, stats-toppling use of the checklist. "So simple it sounds dumb," one of his book reviewers wrote, "until you hear the case for it."

The case for it is that the most highly trained person can skip a step,

---

[6] Atul Gawande, "The Trick to Surviving A High Stakes, High Pressure Job? Try A Checklist," interview by Shankar Vedantam, *Hidden Brain*, NPR, October 30, 2017, audio, 50:00, https://www.npr.org/transcripts/559996276.

overlook a question, forget a critical detail. And that's it. That's the case. In the world of physicians, oversights can be high stakes. But with a little humility, Gawande says in *The Checklist Manifesto: How to Get Things Right*, as we hold ourselves to checklists, our outcomes stabilize and improve.

As late as 2001, more people died every year from catheter infections than from breast or prostate cancer. A catheter is a thin tube inserted into the bladder or a vein. When bacteria get in, the infection can kill, and for years a percentage of catheter deaths seemed inevitable. Then one day the Centers for Disease Control and Prevention issued a checklist for doctors to never overlook mundane and obvious things like washing their hands with soap before inserting a catheter; covering the patient with sterile drapes; wearing gloves, gowns, masks, and so on.

What happened? For starters, physicians didn't like being checked on. And nurses having to double check the physicians didn't like having their heads chewed off. Nurses were ordered to hold their docs to the checklist or be fired. If a physician balked, the nurses were to report it. When checklist compliance rose from 75 to 98 percent, Gawande said, infection rates dropped from five per one thousand "catheter days" to two. For longer-term catheters, a second checklist took infection rates to zero.

In the meantime, those lists also teach.

How much thought have you given to checklists? One of my colleagues, on his home bathroom door, lists everything he needs in a business suitcase. Before he's out the door on a trip, he glances down the list. I have friends who, before a dinner out, draft questions to

RESPOND

draw out true conversation. When we know the recipe but go to it anyway, we're looking for a checklist.

Where are your mundane checklists? In pretty much every sense and form, in business and at home, I'm for them, and not just checklists. I'm for written reminders of the things that lift our lives and help us lift others': in the ways that lists of my skills and priorities help me screen opportunities, in the way I can hold to mundane but important steps, in the ways common lists build uncommon teams, in the ways my written prayers and list of tasks—daily, weekly, monthly, and so on—actually effect change.

I also think that if we could read our lists in reverse, from today to last week, last month, last year, or five years ago, they would rewind to show God's providence.

## COMMIT TO THE DAILY

Earlier in this chapter I confessed (it is a confession) that my mind defaults to the future, something my son, Jake, caught onto early. One day when he was about eleven years old, he said to me, "Dad, yesterday is history. Tomorrow a mystery. And today is a gift. That's why it's called the present."

With a straight face, I hope, I asked if he was quoting Socrates. He said no, *Kung Fu Panda*, and the point stands. The present is a gift, a beautiful tension between all we know and all we can't know. In the Venn diagram of today and tomorrow, the overlap is the healthy tension of our habits, routines, reasoning—all growing in discipline and purpose as we mature in God.

In Psalm 37:5, an elderly and seasoned King David writes, "Commit thy way unto the Lord; trust also in him and he shall bring it to pass" (KJV). In David's words I hear the meekness, the obedience, that sets us free. As we commit our way and loosen our grip, a little becomes enough, and a lot can't own us. Wealth and fame gain perspective; "who you know" loses its starch. Health and suffering become twin teachers of love and goodness; defeat is never defeat. In hard times, we learn calm and trust. In all times, we gain purpose, whether it shows at the time or not.

To commit our way, day by day, is to grasp the Kingdom's upside-down promises that giving is gain, suffering can heal, in helping others we help ourselves, discipline is freedom, and in dying we live. Everything rides on where we commit.

In his book *Ordering Your Private World*, Gordon McDonald reminds us (for me this is another confession) that unseized time flows to our weaknesses. That's not a call to stay busy but a reminder to stay in our strengths. Once we know our callings, even downtime can sharpen our natural gifts instead of losing precious hours in B-level pursuits.

Jesus knew his mission, his human limitations, his political and cultural times. He prepared for thirty years for a three-year ministry. At times he preached to thousands, but more often he poured into private prayer, solitude, a dozen disciples, a handful of friends. Jesus never mistook size for impact.

Readiness is holy ground. We control the things we can control, humbly check our lists, and stay open to opportunity. We find or form the teams that share our visions. At every turn, we commit our way.

And chance favors the prepared life.

RESPOND

# A READINESS LIST

Readiness is stewardship because we're made, as someone has said, with eternity in mind.

1.  **Either know who you are or find out.** To get from success to significance, you have to know yourself.

2.  **Look further to see better.** Early in our careers we can see about four years ahead. Beyond that is mystery. A little success increases our understanding. As our eyes open to options twenty or thirty years ahead, we're clearer about decisions now.

3.  **Determine what you believe.** High achievers tend to know where they stand on life's basic questions.

4.  **Aim high. Aim to make a meaningful life from an ordinary one.** Set your sights on big achievements and set them far enough ahead of your current achievements to make the journey both demanding and worth it.

5.  **Don't overplan.** Opportunity comes in over the transom, not through the door. Make your plans, then stay ready for big change on short notice. In its extreme, planning can deafen us to opportunity, which knocks but once.

6.  **Screen with your values.** Unless you respect your work, not only will you perform poorly, but the work can corrupt and possibly kill. Work by your values. Only you can prevent bad career choices.

7.  **Define what finishing well means for you.** Only you can set your endgame.

8.  **Know your season.** Years and eras, like a sigmoid curve, break into learning, output, and harvest and rest. Accept that work comes in seasons.

9.  **Know the results you want.** Uncertain results come to people unsure of what they want. Good results start with good questions, then in partnerships and teams with expertise, knowledge, and discipline to help you achieve what you have in mind.

10. **Don't stop living.** We reach a point when the next stage will either drain or enrich us. Near the final work stage, we can retire and wither. Or we can stay in our work with diminishing enthusiasm. Or we can stay in our work and find new life as part of something bigger than just ourselves.

## ASK YOURSELF

1. In my life, what does readiness look like?

2. How do I order my days—calendar, lists, and so on—and by what priorities?

3. Life has mundane, repetitive tasks. How do I regard and manage them?

4. What is my attitude toward goals? Do I find them restrictive? Liberating? When has setting goals worked for or against me?

5. What checklist am I overdue to write?

RESPOND

SECTION 3

# RECHARGE

# CHAPTER TEN

# PAUSE TO ADVANCE

*Look. Listen. Rest.*

"Silence is difficult, but it makes a man
able to allow himself to be led by God."

— **Robert Cardinal Sarah,** *The Power of Silence*

RECHARGE

Truman Capote's nonfiction best seller *In Cold Blood* is about four murders in Holcomb, Kansas, my hometown. Anywhere in the world I went with my work, from Kansas City to Tokyo, with any mention of where I grew up, someone would make the connection.

I'd say yes, we knew the Clutters: prosperous farmers, active at school, well liked. Some people said the killers had been in prison with one of Mr. Clutter's former workers. He told them a safe in the Clutters' home was full of money.

Except there was no safe. After brutally murdering the entire family, the former convicts left with $46. A month later police caught up with them states away. Until then, people in Holcomb held their breath, locked their doors, and lived in fear. In most ways we were better for the soul-searching, but we were never the same.

When Lee Harvey Oswald assassinated John Kennedy, when the Space Shuttle Challenger blew up, when terrorists took down the World Trade Center, the time COVID-19 gripped the world . . . just as in Holcomb, before we could move on, we all had to slow for hard questions. "What just happened?" "What's important to us?" "Are there lessons here?" "What now?"

And eventually the question comes up: Why does it take tragedy to bring us to ourselves?

If you're this far into *Plan of Action* and asking what to do next in your life, if you've been spared a tragedy or crisis that makes you turn off the noise to ask hard questions, first, you belong to a small category, and second, why wait for trouble?

For towns and nations, more specifically for the people in them, few things lead us as well as silence—not just quiet, but silence, the time to listen, reflect, and recharge. This chapter is about the pauses we need to think and change. I trust you'll make notes on these pages; I hope you'll put other thoughts in writing.

As with all advice in *Plan of Action*, I hope you will innovate.

## A PAUSE TO WRITE

For years Megan Akin wrote an annual letter to her family. It started after the second baby, when doctors found a lump in her breast. There were things she wanted her kids to know. As a physical therapist, she also saw elderly clients with drifting memories and no mental anchors.

One day she put a notebook in her kitchen. As thoughts came up or the kids said something to remember, she scribbled it down. Until the last of their three children left home, every year during the family's summer vacation in Colorado, she'd find a day to grab the notebook and slip off. For hours on paper she'd comb through the year and say what she and her husband, John, saw for the kids. Back at the cabin with the family, she'd read it aloud. Every letter, she says, helped give purpose to their lives—the kids', especially—for the next year.

Peggy Wehmeyer is a former national television correspondent for ABC's *World News Tonight*. When she was twelve years old and in family turmoil, her diary became a safe room, and she kept up the writing.

"As I grew older and more reflective," she says, "my entries started to read like psalms in the sense that they would begin with lament and lead to praise and understanding. In the first part, I get out

RECHARGE

# THE CAREER PAUSE

Whatever your age or career stage, a pause in your career is not a shutdown or enforced solitude. It's a step into new perspective and renewed joy. You finish a goal, organize a closet, reconnect with a parent or friend.

In Debbie Dellinger's book, a pause is six months to a year. If someone asks what you're doing, she advises, you say you're looking at your options. When you have a decision, you'll let them know.

From years of helping high-level men and women, Debbie describes a career pause as the following.

- **A chance to heal:** It's not a deadline to write a master plan. It's mental space to exhale, decompress, reflect, heal. As much as possible, for essentials like relationships, health, and spirit, the time makes room for new priorities.

- **An invitation to ask:** What do I love? What have I always wanted? Who matters to me? What excites me or gives me joy? What do I never want to do again? Where can I make a difference? (No asking, "What's next?")

- **Free of should:** A "should" is a value judgment. When you're in transition, well-meaning people may suggest something you should do. But you alone can know what works for you.

- **A return to old joys:** When golf is not about business, you may rediscover the joy of playing. Or you pull out your camera. Or from the back of the closet, you retrieve that dusty musical instrument and find a community orchestra.

- **Space to reconnect:** Dust off your good intentions and follow through with people. Every reconnection has something for you.

- **A move to regain health:** Leaders live on call to people, economics, safety, world news, politics, decisions, details, and fluctuations. The price of full-time availability is poor sleep, diet, and exercise. Come back to balance.

- **An option for school:** A young person's gap year puts formal education on hold. The mid- or postcareer pause may do just the opposite. Harvard's postcareer course, for instance, builds around nonprofit impact. Stanford's goes wider. Both are on-campus. Courses, like teams, open us to peers, networking, curiosity, personal insights, and more.

- **A reason to break rules:** Break a few of your rules. Learn exactly where your heart belongs and how to get there.

what no one else needs to see or hear. In the back half, I'm praying and worshiping and hearing from God. I write my praise and gratitude and any wisdom that comes my way."

An attorney I know was just out of law school and facing life decisions when he started a journal "to process clearly the issues in front of [him]." His hybrid of self-examination, prayer, and wisdom from other authors, in long hours in a café or coffee shop, began to clarify his thinking in the light of eternal truth. The act of writing, he says, brought his thoughts together.

Plenty of times the privacy of a spiral-bound notebook is its own end. One mother of a college-age son saw her words run off of him like water. "I was a dripping faucet," she said. "I'd start talking and his eyes would roll, so I'd talk more." In desperation, she poured her worries into her notebook of handwritten prayers. No one saw what she wrote, but through the next year her son's life changed in ways she'd prayed for and in ways she wouldn't have known to pray for.

That's how writing works. In journals, an annual letter, notes on paper, calendar updates . . . in words about days and thoughts otherwise easy to forget, we gain what Jesus called "eyes to see." One exec, after a painful exit from a long-term business partnership, spent months in the psalms. Next to a line or passage that seemed to have his name on it, he'd put that day's date. Six months or a year later, and since—like happening onto altars—he'll see a psalm that sustained him next to a reminder of God's timing.

If you're young, you don't have to be a "writer" to make notes. If you're older and have never jotted thoughts and markers, start today. At any point in life, if self-knowledge improves perspective,

RECHARGE

and it does, seeing ourselves on paper can open shortcuts. Over time, deeper parts of us find a voice. Longstanding walls crack and stones tumble. In a journal, a repeating issue can be a flashing light. Our attitudes show up, unvarnished, sending signals. Space opens for us to safely think.

## A PAUSE TO LISTEN

The scene is this: The Old Testament prophet Elijah, fresh from high-level victory over a mob of false prophets, is fleeing wrongful arrest. He gets to a cave on Mount Sinai and, knowing the Lord will soon pass by, braces to hear God. And God speaks but nothing in the way he expects.

## ⊕ LISTENING PRAYER 101

1. **Sit:** Set a timer for twenty minutes. Sit silently with a Bible or book and a blank notebook, journal, or sheet of paper and pen.

2. **Read:** To begin to dial in, read a passage or paragraph. As you do, if a word or phrase stands out, take note.

3. **Invite:** Ask the Holy Spirit to be present, to help you hear him above your own thoughts.

4. **Write:** Write your prayer on paper and relax. As your mind wanders, and it will, guide yourself back to listening. As thoughts or pictures surface, write them down. You may want to read. If a to-do comes to mind, jot it on a separate sheet and guide yourself back to the moment.

5. **Reflect:** For any thoughts that you write on your paper or journal, ask God to clarify and confirm. Does it echo Scripture? If it seems meaningful but unclear, take it to a mature Christian or trusted spiritual director.

6. **Bask:** Remind yourself how deeply God loves you. Praise him. Amen.

*And behold, the Lord passed by, and a great and strong wind tore into the mountains and broke the rocks in pieces before the Lord, but the Lord was not in the wind. And after the wind an earthquake, but the Lord was not in the earthquake. And after the earthquake a fire, but the Lord was not in the fire. And after the fire the sound of a low whisper.* (1 Kings 19:11–12 ESV)

In a "low whisper," Jeremiah writes in verse 12, Elijah at last hears God.

Rabbi Lord Jonathan Sacks, for twenty years chief rabbi of Great Britain, a theologian of the first order, said God is not in the business of impressing us with his power. "The voice that summoned the universe into being is still and small, hardly louder than a whisper," Rabbi Sacks[7] said. "To hear God you have to listen."

That inner ear matures in solitude and in time; in the twenty-first century this is no small order. It rewards us as we learn to patiently, repeatedly press back against the beeps and signals. As our interior noise dials down, like Elijah we recognize that God speaks on his terms, not ours, and in knowing love.

How do I hear God? Typically, I'm someplace quiet, low on interruptions. Usually, I have paper (a journal helps keep it in one place) and pen. I read or sit, and in the quiet of a pause to listen, I "hear" him in thoughts or mental pictures.

Not every thought, not at once, not every time. Seldom do thoughts come with crystalline clarity. But in making space to con-

---

[7] Rabbi Sacks, "Elijah and the Prophetic Truth of the 'Still, Small Voice'," Rabbisacks. org, July 7, 2007, https://rabbisacks.org/elijah-prophetic-truth-still-small-voice/.

RECHARGE

sider my steps or to unload certain questions or worries, again, with my journal before me and jotting fragments as they come to mind, I tend to leave with a perspective I couldn't have ginned up for myself. Worries lift. A sense of trust spreads, and with it comes hope. People who annoy me, I can love. In situations that tighten my hands and jaw, I can unclench. I don't make things happen, but I'm available to them.

These days I like to think I'm quicker to sense God's voice, though I do well to stay careful. When I'm unsure of something, I test it against Scripture or run it past someone I consider spiritually mature. At a minimum, in listening prayer, my thoughts have gotten off the hamster wheel.

If any part of this tugs at your sleeve, I also recommend outside counsel. Like financial experts, coaches, and therapists, when the relationship works, a spiritual advisor has resources we lack and sees things we can't—and here we find ourselves back to the value of teams.

## THE PAUSE FROM WORK

Why carve space to rest and think? The list of practical reasons starts with your health, your relationships, your peace of mind, your energy, your career, and your personal direction.

On the subject of rest, we owe volumes to our Jewish brothers and sisters. In *The Gift of Rest: Rediscovering the Beauty of the Sabbath*, former US Senator Joe Lieberman explained how bodies and souls are made for regular rest, ceasing all activity. When we have it, he says, our relationships are sweeter, our productivity higher, our health better.

To sanctify means to set apart for higher purpose. The first thing God sanctified, the renowned scholar Abraham Joshua Herschel said, was time. In his classic *The Sabbath: Its Meaning for Modern Man*, Herschel asks what else the universe still needed after the six days of creation.[8] It lacked the harmony of work and rest. Only as God names the Sabbath, a time to cease work, is his work complete.

Our day of rest, Rabbi Herschel says, takes us from the world of creation to the creation of the world. The Randy Linville summary: the crown of our labor is the perspective in our pause.

And yet, how we resist the pause.

At an atypical company called My Next Season, my friend Debbie Dellinger helps high-performance women and men trade corporate work for the nonprofit world. Or not. First, they have to take a break.

Typical My Next Season clients have won in business and lost at home, having sacrificed their families, relationships, health, even their identities. To now need to read a nonbusiness book, or to meditate or take a quiet walk, counters everything they're made for. It's not just that busyness can be a form of denial. It's that they're wired for responsibility, not time off.

But even for corporate rock stars, a day comes when work ends and emails drop off. And the silence is ringing, says Debbie, a veteran of a Fortune Fifty company. Industry titans known for big decisions and crowded calendars suddenly have empty hours. Like Elijah in the rock, they have to listen not for a thunderclap or a roar but a low

---

[8] Abraham Joshua Heschel, *The Sabbath: Its Meaning for Modern Man* (New York: Farrar, Straus and Young, 1951).

RECHARGE

whisper . . . in a book or an article, on a billboard, in a conversation, prayer, a memory. And it's hard.

## THE CONSEQUENCES OF A PAUSE

Meanwhile, the case for pauses surrounds us. Genesis gives us the Sabbath. Later books in the Bible introduce the sabbatical—fields left unplowed every seventh harvest. Dr. Gawande mentions "pause points," when teams come together over a single checklist. Rest, say reports from *Scientific American* to *Inc.*, fuels creativity.[9] In politics, in agriculture, in architecture, in art . . . pauses help us rest from the known and invite the unknown.

Sunday mornings with my *Book of Life*, in and out of prayer, I consider where problems resolved, roadblocks formed bridges, and stuck places gave way. I see principles play out, like the one that says when two parties disagree for a long period, both are wrong. (Or the principle that says when results disappoint, question your methods. Or when an issue repeats, look for the lesson.) With those things top of mind, I move into prayer, which takes me past a wish list to a relationship.

In that pause, my writing gives me perspective. Jake laughs at my use of the word *amalgamation*, but in my prayer notes, simple as they

---

[9] Ferris Jabr, "Q&A: Why a Rested Brain Is More Creative: Taking Breaks—from Naps to Sabbaticals—Can Help Us to Refocus and Recharge," *Scientific American*, September 1, 2016, https://www.scientificamerican.com/article/q-a-why-a-rested-brain-is-more-creative/; Geoffrey James, "Neuroscience: Relaxing Makes You More Creative," *Inc.*, January 12, 2015, https://www.inc.com/geoffrey-james/neuroscience-relaxing-makes-you-more-creative.html.

are, the fragments come together. I check my calendar for last week and next, for different teams, for projects. I update. I may review the same period in previous years. I may go back to other prayers in that period in those years. I write, and my thinking begins to flow. The payoff has something to do with courage because the increasing clarity hits reset for the coming week.

To look and to see better, to learn to hear God, to make time for what multiplies our time—can it hurt to try?

Go for the clarity that only rest can bring. Shut off your electronics. Allow for mistakes. Keep in mind that no good thing is a one-off. As Aristotle said, we are what we repeatedly do.

## ASK YOURSELF

1. How do I form or improve my perspective? How—or how not—does my journal or any kind of notes I keep inform my perspective?

2. Do I believe it's possible to know God's will? How do I believe I hear God?

3. Do I resist solitude? Why or why not?

4. In my life, what difference would it make to also be rested? How can I make that happen?

5. What is a simple way to begin to add time for silence to my days?

RECHARGE

# CHAPTER ELEVEN

# PAY WISDOM FORWARD

*Leave More Than Silence*

In teaching others we teach ourselves.

**— Traditional proverb**

RECHARGE

T he early years in my supply-chain career were at Pillsbury, the ag industry's Mount Olympus, headwaters of top traders in the nation. As a freshman trader there, I learned under a handful of senior managers who trained by teams and taught by checklists.

One of those lists, wryly titled "Lessons Learned & Sometimes Followed," suited up life wisdom as industry advice, and it was legend. Simple and concise, it left room for human fallacy but no doubt about the behaviors and disciplines necessary to master time zones, morning news, and hunches. The value-adds were several bloodstained industry proverbs that trainees like me would still have to mature into. Take a line like "Short crops have a long tail." What does that mean? It means when a crop is lean one year, prices for that commodity spike and owners ration the supply. So a bad harvest has a longer shelf life.

As interns migrated through Pillsbury's various departments, so did the checklist. As traders filtered out through the industry, so did the checklist. When I left, I shared it with my new coworkers. Somewhere through the years I lost track of the list, but during the writing of this book a longtime associate and friend sent me his copy, now in the appendix.

What is it that makes us want to share wisdom or to see it when others do? Examples stretch from the book of Proverbs in the Bible to college commencement speeches to a list of treasures like *Tuesdays with Morrie, Man's Search for Meaning, Twelve Rules for Life,* and *Seven Habits of Highly Effective People.* Memoirs can be another form of wisdom literature. And books and letters by dying men and women—*The Last Lecture* comes to mind—clear a path through the clutter to teach or remind us what matters.

In a salute to the wisdom around us, this chapter draws from my career-and-life stockpile of hit-the-wall insights, war wounds, scavenged brilliance, borrowed gems—from my list, so far, of some fifty pieces. Writing and reading them for this chapter, and sharing them with family and others, I get the sense again of passing a baton in a relay.

Why make my own list? For the same reason I read, journal, and pray. Because my hold on life-guiding truths, like nutrition and communication devices, always need recharging. And because wisdom fascinates me.

The obvious subtext to all of this is for you to write your list. This chapter invites you to start your own.

A friend of mine at Anheuser-Busch once boarded a plane in Lynchburg with a first draft of twenty-five life lessons. By the time the plane touched down in Kansas City, he had seventy-five. This man is the exception. Most of us come to our life insights—once we turn our minds to it—in time and by degrees. I know because while writing this chapter, over coffee or meals out, I'd ask friends for their lessons. Eyes would drift off and I'd hear, "No one's ever asked," or some variation of "hmm." So I'd prod. "What do your kids or staff say you always say?" At that point, some ideas might sputter and start. "My kids tell me I say . . ."

In Dallas, Robin Blakeley, a dad of four sons, noticed several standout students at his kids' school and found out they were all brothers. Robin's a guy who does more than observe. He took the boys' father to lunch and asked for parenting advice.

RECHARGE

# THE LEADERSHIP CHECKLIST

As a CEO I oversaw a team of teams, a hundred-plus frontline managers all heading groups from small to companywide. Each person had to be able to say, "Leadership starts with me." In the spirit of Pillsbury's "Lessons Learned," I wanted my teams to have a snapshot list of a leader's essential qualities and skills. After a few years of polishing, under four headings that also teach, here is that list:

## Set Up for Success

1. Look for trends that drive strategy.

2. Keep in mind that plans are nothing, planning is everything.

3. Know what to do, how to do it, and for whom.

4. Know the factors critical to success.

## Build the Culture

1. Establish common understandings, beliefs, and values.

2. Walk your talk in your own behavior.

## Lead Your People

1. Understand your own behavior and develop yourself to manage yourself.

2. Know or learn how to manage resources and build the culture.

3. Learn to lead people, develop leaders, and create a high-performance environment.

## Continue to Learn

1. Communicate and seek feedback and input.

2. Think and act both globally and locally.

3. Validate what you know and identify things to learn.

Predictably, the man's first response was a stare, but through the meal, Robin got gold. *Take your sons camping. Leave the devices at home and sit under the night sky. Pull a boy into your lap and talk about who made the stars. Give affectionate and strong nicknames like Bear Cub or Warrior. Treat your wife as you want your boys to treat their future wives. Keep popcorn and sleeping bags on hand; when friends want to stay over, always say yes. You'll know the friends and your kids. At night, as you pray for each of your boys, lay your hands on their heads.*

Robin's LinkedIn page is small as those pages go, but the "fathering boys" list, when he posted it, drew more than ten thousand hits.

Two things are true: every person is one of a kind, and nothing is new under the sun. Additionally, we grow as we give. Each of us, whether intentionally, processes events and has conclusions to share.

Will you start your own list? Just the making of it, I can guarantee, will reshape your awareness. Our lists also stand to affect others. In the way we wish we'd written down the things our children said, the day comes when we're sorry to have forgotten so much of what our parents told us.

My list below, compiled for this book, reads like modern-day parables. That's not mandatory for your list. Your only job, as I repeatedly say, is to innovate. Start writing. If our wealth in life is wisdom—and it is—it matters that we leave the world with more than silence.

## 1. THE TEN-YEAR RULE

For years I was in a Bible study with Sean Miller, part of a family with a well-known business in Kansas City. One day, when

RECHARGE

Sean's dad was in his mid-eighties, admired and still active, he came along to the study and quickly became the center of our attention. Before closing, someone asked him for lessons from his life. Mr. Miller may have given several that day, but I remember his ten-year rule. *If it won't matter in ten years, it doesn't matter now.*

Words that simple can sound like a platitude. But this Paul Bunyan of our community knew hardship, business struggles, civic burdens, and family challenges. If ten years can improve the view, why stop there? When I'm down or up, if I can glimpse the day from eternity, every valley or mountain tends to adjust to scale.

*Perspective changes things. Eternal perspective is everything.*

## 2. SEIZE THE SURPRISE

On our short list of favorite vacation photos is one of Jake at an Irish archery range. He's retrieving his arrow from a bull's-eye. If he'd been aiming at a different target, you'd also have my picture of how business development works.

In business we set our plans, allow for challenges, pull back, and *zzzzt*: surprise hit. Through my career, more curious to me than our well-planned scores were how many companies, and people, rejected any hit outside their capital-P Plan.

Remember Eisenhower's saying, "Plans are useless; planning is everything"? Actual events seldom match our best-laid plans, but because of the planning, we're more ready to seize the surprise.

*Respect the unexpected.*

## 3. GET OUT OF YOUR WAY

Once there was a middle manager who managed everything. Even office upgrades like chairs, rugs, and paintings. In all that can-do overdo, he may also have been colorblind because his design choices seemed to run the spectrum from beige to gray.

This manager ignored his weakness. Two kinds of people can wreck projects: those who sit on a skill and say nothing, often from misplaced humility, and those who see a deficiency as something to grind through. The second weakness starts in high school, I'm convinced, when GPAs train us to strengthen our shortcomings and shortchange our strengths. We enter work with no sense of how to delegate for balance, how to stay out of our own way.

The point is to build on areas of personal strengths and reduce the potential harm of your weaknesses.

Or just this: *When time matters, do what you do best.*

## 4. BROKEN WINDOWS, BLURRED LINES

In 1968 I was a small, skinny, high school freshman, a no-growth wonder walking the halls with senior athletes, several of them six-foot-three or taller, all of them having a banner year. At fourteen I was old enough to know the rules, young enough to struggle when they blurred.

One night that fall, rocks broke school windows, and the culprits were four of our top players. Other students would have been kicked out of school, but our sports record that year teetered on historic and these were all-sports athletes. The four vandals stood

RECHARGE

before the student body and apologized. That was it. As basketball season began, they sat out several games.

For this ninth grader, right and wrong went dim. Giants in my world damaged property, but what would have happened to less-gifted offenders? In my three decades of management, when I've had to uphold policy, those scenes come back to me.

The story is told and retold of UCLA's legendary basketball coach John Wooden when his new headline center, Bill Walton, showed up with nonregulation facial hair. The year was 1971, and the beard, Walton said, was his right to self-expression.

Coach Wooden told Walton he admired people who had strong beliefs and stuck by them. He said the team would miss him. An *LA Times* reporter wrote at Coach's passing, "Twenty minutes later, Walton was so clean shaven he could have made a commercial for any razor company in the world."

We test standards; that's what humans do. But the best things happen when the standards test us.

*Policies tell but consistency shows.*

## 5. ACTUARIES ON PURPOSE

More than exercise, supplements or diet, what lengthens our lives, researchers say, is purpose.[10] Pair that with the message in a small book titled *Man's Search for Meaning*, on the Library of Congress's list of our country's

---

[10] Kashmira Gander, "People With a Sense of Purpose Live Longer, Study Suggests," *Newsweek*, May 24, 2019, https://www.newsweek.com/people-sense-purpose-live-longer-study-suggests-1433771.

ten most influential books. In World War II death camps the book's author, Viktor Frankl, a psychiatrist and a prisoner, studied the men around him. The ones most likely to endure, he said, were fueled not by anger but by hope. They had something or someone to get back to.

*Between resentment and hope, choose life.*

## 6. TRUTH AND LOVE

When Grace and Jake were little and testing us, I'd laugh and say kids outgrow it. *Just love 'em.* But in Debbie's book, love is discipline, and where I winked, she drew lines. (Evidence quickly backed Debbie as the smallest Linvilles first crawled, then ran and leapt into every flaw and fallacy of the human condition.)

At work, meanwhile, I was all discipline. "To be realistic," I'd say in a meeting or review. I'd slice to the issue regardless of who was left bleeding.

When I learned to pair truth with love—to praise at least four times as much as I criticized—everything about my work improved. Truth alone can wound. Sentiment alone may conceal. Truth in love builds lives and loyalty.

*Be hard on issues, soft on people.*

## 7. THE PHILLIPS CURVEBALL

In 2019 the Federal Reserve and the Trump administration invalidated the Phillips curve, a longstanding theory that unemployment and inflation move in inverse directions. Since grad school, I'd

RECHARGE

known that top economists used the Phillips curve to gauge national and global trends. As I write, unemployment and inflation are on parallel tracks and a once bedrock principle is consigned to history. This is a spot-on illustration of what I call the validate principle.

*Even when the rule is airtight, validate what you know; identify what you still need to learn.*

# 8. BIGGER SLICE, BIGGER PIE

"When do you have enough?" The day I heard that question, I had financial security to my collarbone and "enough" had never come up. That day it struck me that to fully invest in others I'd have to say "when" for myself. No fuel, no mission.

My financial independence would run on passive income, I decided, which requires financial planning, which most people love as much as election years and root canals. But planning is the line between accounting and finance. One colors inside the box; the other builds a box. Accounting is pie slicing; financial planning can make bigger, better, longer-lasting pies—not on a spreadsheet or with more hours but with people and research and ideas and risk.

The summer after my freshman year in high school, my friends found jobs and Dad gave me a field. My buddies earned wages and time off; my job description was to plant, harvest, and sell. By late fall, I knew my life income would never be by the hour.

So two questions: What is enough for you? And how can you plan to be on mission and fuel it?

*Accounting colors inside the box. Financial planning builds a new box.*

## 9. BEAT THE FUNERAL

During my tenure as a CEO, a popular member of our board died, and his wife asked me to speak at his funeral. Knowing too little of this man outside of our meetings, I asked around.

One leader in our company said his eyes had been level with the world, meaning everyone was his equal. Our founder called him "the father of the spirit of the company." I knew he was as good as his word. And I'd long mused on his remark to me once that burial pants have no pockets; we take only ourselves.

What I couldn't say was whether this man knew of the groundswell of love and respect for him. I resolved then, especially for business colleagues, never to withhold praise, never to wait for the funeral to honor someone. In the same spirit, if someone gives you a compliment, honor the giver and accept it.

*Don't wait for the funeral to express love.*

## 10. IF IT'S EASY, KEEP LOOKING

In the sink-or-swim world of supply chain ag, I was blessed by an early shove into the deep end. My desk at Pillsbury was a daily firehose of decisions too big for someone so young, and it almost undid me. But if I were to prescribe a career path now, I'd say to interview with companies too big and too busy to babysit, the kind where a little talent only brings on a new pile. Because next thing you know, you've mastered something. And yes, it's scary. And what's your point?

*Try to make every goal at least one size too big.*

RECHARGE

## 11. BUILD YOUR BRAND

Every company has a brand. Every brand is as good as the general faith in it, and brand faith can be fragile. Some employee makes a mess of customer service, and suddenly you're defined by your worst day.

Our personal brand is our name, our reputation. The bible's book of Proverbs ranks it above gold. As a first-time manager I learned how names rise and fall. People might forget an exact promise but not the follow-through. My words might waft into the ether, but my deeds had an extended shelf life.

Every day, day after day . . . that day is all we have.

*Live each day as if your name depends on it.*

## 12. TRY SOMETHING ELSE

Remember the woman whose teenage son ignored her? She'd talk. He'd roll his eyes. She'd talk more. One day she rechanneled her worries into a private prayer notebook. Through the next year her son's life changed in ways far beyond her power to will or to wheedle.

One moral is if it's not working, try something else. In business multiply that by ten. Before you become a dinosaur, audit your habits. Change. Adapt. Always be learning. If insanity is repeating the same act expecting a new result, then for goodness' sake innovate.

The young challenge every assumption. The mature must learn to challenge even their own experience. Where do the two meet? In relationship and talk. We visit each other's worlds without judgment, and we stay open.

*If it's not working, try something else.*

While I was working on this chapter, my family and I were in Beaver Creek, Colorado, just west of Vail. Summers there are slow, and one day as we strolled through a few shops everyone in the group seemed to be finding collectibles. Clowns. Impressionist art. Birds. Outside a store, my sister asked me what I collect, and half thinking, I answered, "Nothing."

My wife, Debbie, broke in. "Not true," she said. "He collects memories and ideas."

That is true. From a career of checklists and policies, after decades of finding ways to build and unify people and teams and a company, when I come across good stuff—a concept, an insight, some innovation—my reflex is to write it down, consider it, get it to people who can use it.

Not because there's so much to know but because we forget so much we already know.

## ASK YOURSELF

1. What advice has served me most? What do my kids, friends, or coworkers say I always say?

2. Who's been a model in my life, and how? (Which people do I quote or copy?)

3. What wisdom do I carry in my mind?

4. If all I could leave in my will was three pieces of wisdom, advice, or lessons learned, what would they be?

5. Of what benefit is it to write down what I've learned and how I learned it?

RECHARGE

# CHAPTER TWELVE

# PRACTICE GRATITUDE

*Of Masters, Mentors, and Peers*

"I would maintain that thanks are
the highest form of thought,
and that gratitude is happiness
doubled by wonder."
— **G. K. Chesterton**

RECHARGE

W hen the time came, my father gave me my future and not his.

I was at the end of my senior year in high school. My brother, Stan, was still in middle school. Dad could have kept me in a nearby junior college and used me part-time. Never mind that I missed details because my head was other places. Or that I liked working with people and was good at persuasion and at schoolwork. Or that livestock judging had showcased my decision-making skills.

These days it's well known that 70 percent of family-owned businesses end in second-generation wreckage. Ten percent make it to generation three. What Dad knew was that aptitude matters and that bloodline can't square a person's gifts to a need at hand.

And he knew me. That final spring of high school my sport was track and field. I was as strong and fast as I'd ever be, and we'd had a good season. My plan was to get a scholarship, play small-school athletics, and get into coaching. In early May Dad told me to hang up my track shoes and move on with studies.

Did I resent his direction? It was a rush. By nature he led for the flourishing of those around him. He released me to go to school six hours east in Manhattan, Kansas, where I'd major in ag econ, a field I knew. Down the line I'd add business finance.

From the far end of my career, I see my father now as able to lead past himself. I bring it up because in decades of buying companies, I saw family businesses squash their young by pushing genetics over personal choice. The Belgian family firm in chapter 7, the one in its sixth generation, busted the stats precisely because its leaders knew to temper DNA with competence.

# CLEAR-EYED PRAISE

This brings us to gratitude, not rose-tinted sentimentality but a clear-eyed nod to the people whose lives have advanced ours. Practically speaking, gratitude is a portal to the real world, bad and good, and a roadmap to finding and getting the best.

In practice, gratitude is specific. It names names.

In Washington, DC, the United States Holocaust Memorial Museum tells its stories through specific people with real names, not just of Jewish victims. To move through the exhibits, you're issued a passport of a real person from the crisis years. Through the displays and the events, if a shop owner hid Jewish neighbors, you're told the owner's name. If an official profited by evil, here is the official's name.

Sports halls of fame trade in specific names. The Vietnam War Memorial in Washington, DC, name by name, frames a generation of sacrifice.

I can't give you every reason to name the people who have elevated your life. I can't tell you why to have it in writing. But I hope this chapter persuades you to do it. In thinking, writing, and rewriting about these people, we reaffirm the ideas of honor, of what's possible, and what to look for. Gratitude as a habit fortifies how we make choices and puts an end to self-pity. (For that alone, it's worth it.)

Gratitude nourishes our souls in ways far beyond what we can know.

# GRATITUDE AND MENTAL HEALTH

I'm backed on this by an exploding field of studies. At Indiana University, to name one, researchers asked whether gratitude

RECHARGE

might lower the school's expenses for psychotherapy.[11] Of the entering students who signed up for counseling, most for depression and anxiety, three hundred were divided into groups of one hundred each. Everyone got therapy. Students in the second group also wrote a weekly letter of gratitude (mailing optional). The third group, besides therapy, journaled weekly about their negative experiences.

Are you sitting down? Compared to the students who journaled their hurt or the ones in counseling only, the ones who wrote out their gratitude reported significant mental improvement. Weeks later the effects lingered.

When we suffer a wrong, great or small, we nurse it to our own injury. In divorce, death, betrayals, insults, gossip, the counterintuitive way out is to forgive and find reasons to be grateful. This isn't Pollyanna talking, it's your actuary table. Optimistic people live longer and better.[12] And optimism is a muscle.

## THE GRIEVANCE MISFIRE

In my lifetime I've seen grievance and resentment politics raised to a fine art and a deadly indulgence, far afield from President Kennedy's call to "ask not what your country can do for you, but what you can

---

[11] Joshua Brown and Joel Wong, "How Gratitude Changes You and Your Brain," *Greater Good Science Center*, June 6, 2017, https://greatergood.berkeley.edu/article/item/how_gratitude_changes_you_and_your_brain.

[12] Patti Neighmond, "Optimists For The Win: Finding The Bright Side Might Help You Live Longer," *Shots*, NPR, September 1, 2019, audio, 2:00, https://www.npr.org/sections/health-shots/2019/09/01/755185560/optimists-for-the-win-finding-the-bright-side-might-help-you-live-longer.

do for your country." Meanwhile, two billion people in the rest of the world can't claim a change of clothes or say where their next meal is coming from. When grievance graduates to a movement of any stripe, I see power seekers more eager to avenge their resentment than to work for life, liberty, and the pursuit of happiness for all.

In the corporate world, grievance shows up in bottom lines. So does its antidote: gratitude. I doubt you'll come across "gratitude" in a business lexicon, but a few pages before the word *morale*, you might find *engagement*. An engaged company knows its success turns on its people. Bonuses show engagement. Listening does. Public recognition does. Public praise is four to five times more productive than a private reprimand. (I believe in personal notes. I hand-signed bonus checks with personal notes of gratitude that many people, I'm told, have kept.)

For their part, employees know who cares. You can conduct an organizational health assessment and see who "kisses up and kicks down" and who treats their people right. Engagement—*gratitude*— shows in the scores and plays out in production.

Gratitude changes our physical chemistry. A woman I know endured a difficult hospital stay with the help of a daily gratitude journal. "You want to give in to worry and fear," she says. "Then you write down, 'I'm grateful we got this doctor. I'm grateful for an earlier appointment with the specialist. I'm grateful to hear from friends.'" In the COVID-19 pandemic one man's gratitude journal helped him give up time with his grandchildren and holiday meals with the extended family.

I know the lure of anger. We all do. Anyone with a pulse can justify some resentment. But the longer we nurse our wounds,

RECHARGE

the more they own us. Our path to freedom passes through forgiveness (again and again) and gratitude. Not for wrongs suffered, though we can value any new empathy we've gained, but for the many rights always born of the wrongs in a world we know is broken.

## NAMING NAMES

The roll call below is an exercise in gratitude that turned into a personal hall of fame. *Of course* I would make a list. Eventually, I labeled the categories "masters, mentors, and peers"—loftier-sounding than "leaders, teachers, and friends." This particular list is polished because I realized I wanted it in this book. Whatever your list looks like, and however you describe the people who added to your life, the point is to make it your own.

Why do it? Why use up time you could otherwise spend on Facebook or watching a movie? Do it and then you tell me. Because it elevates your soul and body. Because it opens your eyes, enlarges your heart, sharpens your focus. *Start your list.* That's all.

One final thing: everything about my list below supports the research. Just from thinking through these people and their gifts to me, whether they knew it or not, the energy and joy I gain are a best-kept secret to life.

## MY MASTERS

After Dad, three people in my life stand out for teaching me leadership on the job. I saw the strengths and tactics in their lives and innovated into mine. Two of them, Matt Rose and Doug Sims, ran what amounts to powerhouse national institutions. The third, Jay Bennett, headed a law firm and two nonprofits. In their spheres, where singleness of purpose is everything, all three were human bonding agents.

**Matt Rose: IQ *and* EQ**. About the time I began to lead my company, Matt, young by CEO standards, was handed leadership of one of North America's seven class-one railways. For a hundred thousand employees and thousands of miles of US tracks, I saw Matt face down weather, deadlines, economics, politics, geography, safety, and chance—and love it.

Most people in the ag world believe every railroad's unwritten client-service motto is "Like it or lump it." So for Matt to make an advisory board of his top customers, like Lincoln's "team of rivals," was groundbreaking. Matt is a railroad worker's son, a graceful multitasker with a practical IQ and an exceptional EQ (emotional maturity). My full term on his board was a front-row seat to use of scope, scale, impact, even difficulty, to head off problems and innovate ideas.

**Doug Sims: clean lines.** Doug's lead in saving rural-American utilities and farm credit traces directly to his clarity in word and deed. I was still a new CEO when his company became part of our credit line. A beat later I was on the FarmHouse board of trustees, and there was Doug at the helm.

Doug was tall and husky. His booming baritone voice sounded like first place in an FFA officer speaking contest. But he did more than talk. He was Mr. Make-It-Happen. When the FarmHouse board he inherited gave him mostly academics, *boom*, he had innovators and entrepreneurs.

RECHARGE

As for clarity I remember Doug's close to our first comprehensive board meeting. From hours of wide-ranging talk, he winnowed to a few pertinent ideas, and every person felt heard. He was masterful.

**Jay Bennett: mystery and wonder.** Jay is a law firm partner and a pragmatist. Yet from the way he steered two faith-based boards, I learned in every project to also factor in mystery and wonder.

One time the board was setting up long-term partnerships. Every pending connection looked like an obvious fit, but they weren't happening. And Jay trusted that. Where we saw walls, he saw a bridge to something as yet unknown. Having done our part, we allowed for forces that no one could anticipate or control.

Jay's radar was set for "more than here, more than now." I saw him assume nothing, ask hard questions, read books, and free discussions to go to unforeseen places. With humor and fun, always gently, he pushed us to launch future good, selflessly planting ideas that next generations would harvest.

## MY MENTORS

For a season or a reason, certain people bring us some knowledge, competence, and virtue—or some combination. Your list may include parents, family members, scout leaders, a friend's parents, a boss, a youth group leader. Part of the fun is tracing the origins of some of our qualities.

**Dean Erwin: discipline.** I've mentioned Coach Erwin before. In high school in Holcomb, Kansas, he coached basketball and taught human physiology. On the court, he taught from the socks up. In class, he made us learn notetaking, something no teenager willingly sets out to master. But I'm grateful I did. Basketball lasted four seasons, but the notetaking, through a career of complex information, enabled me to hear, organize, and process.

**Al Maddux: networking.** Unrelated to high school activities, a county extension agent named Al Maddux formed a livestock judging team that I had the good fortune to join. In barns and livestock centers, in diners, on long car rides, he saw to it that we learned to analyze, decide, and persuade against a ticking clock. To be sure, Mr. Maddux didn't teach us so much as connect us to university profs and professional experts, to high achievers, to specialists in their fields. Mr. Maddux taught me how genuine passion, and sharing it, can open doors.

**Don Brummer: simplicity.** Don, assembler of the famous "Lessons Learned & Sometimes Followed," as his list-making suggests, moved through life creating order and simplicity. In the ag industry in the 1980s and '90s, as international trade changed, supply-chain businesses merged, and systems collided, Don untied knots and kept the work on a human scale. His "management by walking around" paid off in firsthand intel and widespread loyalty. Because of him, I am a list-maker and a better thinker.

**Adam Hamilton: faith.** Not long after Dad's sudden death, Pastor Hamilton introduced me to the spiritual disciplines of Scripture reading, prayer, worship, and other life-giving habits. Through major milestones in my life and work, from our adopting Grace and Jake to my exit from my career, Pastor Hamilton either taught me about God's resources or got me to them.

**Jeff Kirby: theology.** In the 1990s, a pastor-scholar named

RECHARGE

Jeff Kirby, a figure in the global Alpha program, led our churchwide discipleship program, and I got to be there. If Pastor Hamilton set the table with the spiritual disciplines, Jeff filled my plate with applications. He showed me how the disciplines play out in the dailiness of life. Bright, dynamic, seasoned in hard issues, he gave me practical paths to eternal truths.

## MY PEERS

Our peers come wrapped in common interests flavored by other educations and backgrounds. Professionally, our expertise matches. You know you're with a peer when the student–teacher thing goes both ways.

In this list, Butch and I shared a wild ride in the ag industry. Jeff Kirby (see my list of mentors) and Stan Wallace exposed me to faith in daily issues and academia as I shared my thinking, strategy, and leadership. Brad Clark and I, iron and iron, are harnessing business ideas to serve world need.

**Duane Fischer: inspiration.** For nearly ten years, Duane "Butch" Fischer was a friend in the industry and a sometimes competitor. I watched him rise to the top in his company; then I joined it and reported to him. When crisis hit, the future of our company rode on our mutual trust, and we had it. Butch spread courage and fun; he gave and got his stakeholders' best. When he left the helm and I took over, many an important initiative had started with him. I saw him aim for hearts and minds and get much more in return.

**Stan Wallace: significance.** Professors who believe, especially in developing countries, often are alone and unsupported. Dr. Stan

Wallace's Global Scholars creates peer societies for Christian profs to grow professionally and spiritually. Scientists meet scientists; MBAs meet MBAs; all boats rise. Stan opened my eyes to a vast need and far-reaching opportunity. I was privileged to help develop the society and its fourteen impressive services to Christians in the academy.

**Clayton Smith: purpose.** For a raft of reasons, most churches overlook how faith works in business. Enter Clayton Smith, our church's executive pastor, an expert in generosity and stewardship. I once brought Clayton to a small success-to-significance event, and he brought the idea to our church. Avoiding groupthink, Clayton helps professionals of any age find faith, dreams, purpose, and meaning in their work. His book, *Crossroads*, inspired this book.

**Brad Clark: partnership.** In the "iron sharpens iron" column, Brad and I independently left the corporate world to serve nonprofits. When we found each other, we found our functional complements. I'm corporate strategy. He's a serial entrepreneur and a corporate Swiss army knife. Together we're building Triquetra, an investment model adding business savvy to world need, still a marvelous work in progress.

## REVERSE-ENGINEERED VIRTUES

Here are two truths: One, when choices abound, the best strategy is to choose well. Two, we seldom actually choose the people who influence us. At the same time, it's helpful to identify what to look for. Especially when the best people, seeking no attention, tend to stay below the radar.

RECHARGE

With the qualifier that no one is perfect, especially yours truly, reverse-engineering from my masters, mentors, and peers, here are qualities to look for.

**Masters are leaders** who are grownups, not petty or vengeful. They have self-control and lead by serving. Bad news doesn't faze them; good news spurs new ideas. Change is another stimulant. Masters are solid in their faith, families, and communities. They can express what they believe and what they believe in. As needed, they'll take heat for doing what's right. They have the vision thing, and their teams rise on it. While others focus on tasks, heads down, masters' heads are up, erect, and "looking around corners."

**Mentors are teachers** who help us develop world-class skills. Their love for their expertise is infectious, and they're liberal with their time, especially for an eager learner. Where masters are looking down the road, mentors have an eye to the next generation. Professionalism shows in their excellence, year after year. They pursue their own top form, and they want it for others. A good mentor encourages not with sentiment or flattery but with truth in love.

**Peers are friends** who sharpen us in ways few others can. The original sparks fly, C. S. Lewis said, with the words, "You too? I thought I was the only one." Our best friends share our journey. Common interests open the door, then our different backgrounds take us further. Good friends are first of all good people: faithful spouses, parents, neighbors, and citizens. They think for themselves, avoiding groupthink. They are life learners, ever upping their standards. A friend sticks around in matters large and small. A friend has your back.

## ASK YOURSELF

1. Who are just three people I'm grateful for?

2. In my life, what role did each of those people play? Because of them, what do I have that I might have learned later or missed altogether?

3. Have I ever made time to thoughtfully thank someone important to me? Why or why not? If yes, what was the result?

4. In a grievance I deservedly feel right now, however painful, what is something I'm also grateful for?

5. As a master, mentor, or peer, how do I want to be remembered?

RECHARGE

# CONCLUSION

"In their hearts humans plan their course,
but the Lord establishes their steps."

**— Proverbs 16:9**

I was in grade school when my dad's dad, a World War I vet, succumbed to years of health problems, most of them stemming from the war. For Grandma Linville's part, now alone, she used her independence to timeshare life with her six living kids, on both coasts and in the Midwest.

I remember going to pick up Grandma at the Santa Fe Railroad terminal in Garden City. Standing on the platform with Mom, we'd scan for a tiny woman (barely five feet tall) in a hat. In her arms would be the large family scrapbook that went everywhere she went, begun, best I recall, when her first sons left for World War II.

Grandma's scrapbook was family legend. All of us were in it: she and Grandpa, their four sons and three daughters, their sixteen grandkids, and the next generation of spouses. In Grandma's weeks or months with a family, she used the time to update.

And did we pore through the updates. Before Instagram and Facebook were words, clippings and snapshots informed and connected us. If a cousin married, in went a photo. If someone divorced, Grandma deleted. A few items might need explaining, but she had us. "Grandma, what are they doing? Who is this?"

In the fifteen years of Grandma's family circuit and encyclopedic family chronicle, I absorbed the notion that our stories tell us who we are. A bulging scrapbook framed the Linville narrative. Across two wars and a depression, marriages and deaths, state lines and decades, we belonged to something bigger than ourselves. As life decisions arose, certain things were understood.

# REBOOT, RESOLVE, RESPOND, RECHARGE

Every family has low points, tragedies, mistakes, and misunderstandings, but they work for us too. The baseline is to know our stories and, where we don't know them, to fill in the blanks. I hope you'll do it. My prayer is that this book helps.

You may be in or out of college, midcareer, or winding one down—or retired and searching. You may feel depleted, out of touch with no sense of passion or how to know or appreciate your gifts, skills, and desires. You can recover and recharge, and your story is part of it.

If you've lost your dreams, lean into the section in this book called "Reboot." Rediscover what's in your head and heart. Pray. By all means pray. Expose yourself to books, quotes, conversations . . . put yourself in the way of wisdom.

Have I made it clear that *Plan of Action* may be read in any order? Dip into wisdom and gratitude. Consider your gifts and resources. As thoughts surface, write them down. Your pages eventually will talk back to you. As you reclaim pieces of yourself, as you're increasingly able to affirm how you're made, what you love, what you value, where you find meaning . . . protect your yes with an equally strong no.

No one goes it alone. There are people eager to help your dreams come to life. Many of them are in teams, groups, and organizations. You'll be amazed who knows whom, who knows what—all parts of the mystery and wonder. So take risks. Learn to appreciate the gifts of dead ends and surprises. Build on daily disciplines and prepare for the unexpected. When opportunities come, you'll be ready.

# FORTY HARVESTS

In our twenties we're like the young farmer who's handed a parcel of land and looking at forty harvests. He knows his seasons and the cadence. As a nation, we've left the farm, but every life still comes in seasons. And eventually a final season comes.

My single message is this: Don't wait to know God or yourself. Certainly don't fear either one. The One who made you is far easier on you, has far more for you than you know to want. Seek him and find yourself. In his work, for-profit or not, you'll find your purpose. The more we lean on him, surrender into him, the straighter we stand.

And the straighter we stand, the more inclined we are to kneel and thank the One who made us for this journey from success to significance to surrender.

# APPENDICES

# THE TOOLBOX

## THE DAILY WALK
## FROM DREAMS TO REALITY

From decades in business and the nonprofit world, and from years as a student of life, below is my checklist for intentional living. I say it's my checklist . . . the organization is mine, but the contents are broadly tested, far beyond just me or my times. Should any part of this strike you as comfortable and familiar, you may not have read correctly. Collectively and individually, the insights here, and their disciplined pursuit, adapted to you and your life, stand to change everything.

### DAILY

- Learn to pray.
- Master the daily.

### SUNDAY

- Pause to advance.
- Practice gratitude.

### MONTHLY

- Focus.
- Go together.
- Be bold.

### QUARTERLY

- Innovate.
- Pay wisdom forward.

### ANNUAL

- Dream again.
- Choose.
- Be intentional.

# LESSONS LEARNED BUT SELDOM FOLLOWED

## (CIRCA 1988)

*The cheapest part of a crop is usually the tail. As mentioned in chapter 11, to the uninitiated, the guidelines below from Pillsbury in the 1980s—then a mecca for the country's top traders—make little sense. For rookie traders like me, cutting our teeth on buying and selling, this list was a wealth of seasoned insight, a checklist of experience, a mentor on a page. Even a layperson can find timeless counsel. Best practices often come out of bad practices, meaning someone else paid the price and we get the wisdom. I never take that for granted.*

- Take what the market gives you.

- Do what the market tells you to do.

- Carrying charges on grain inventory are only earned in forward sales.

- Do the opposite of the crowd.

- When the small guy gets in, it's time to get out.

- Don't get in the way of a bull or bear market; the trend is your friend.

- The cheapest part of the crop is usually the tail.

- Always sell rallies when in a long position.

- Offer grain into the market every day when long.

- When markets invert, it usually means the basis has gone high enough.

- When freight is high, don't forget to sell destination-market premiums.

- Trading new crops before they are planted is risky.

- When you have good margins, go to the bank with them.

- Don't be in a long position for the time periods that farmers normally clear out bins or seasonally sell.

- Don't be in a short position for the opening of the upper-river navigation season at depressed wintertime basis levels.

- High interest rates create lack of nearby demand.

- Always have some sales on for nearby shipment in carry markets.

- Don't chase the market; it's better to buy dips and sell rallies.

- Get short when the market is high and long when the market is low.

- Do what makes sense to you, not what your competition is doing.

- Cost of freight and destination markets move in the same directions.

- Do not release unsold barges for shipment on the river.

- Short crops usually have long tails.

- When you're wrong, your first loss may be your cheapest way out.

- The words that don't apply to the grain business are *always* and *never*.

# CURATED QUOTES

This is my collection, ever a work in progress, of words initially on a page and now, from frequent readings, in my life.

## FROM GOD'S WORD

*Note: Most translations are from the New International Version (NIV) of the Bible. Some, as indicated, speak best in another translation.*

## ON ENCOURAGEMENT

- "I pray that the eyes of your heart may be enlightened in order that you may know the hope to which he has called you, the riches of his glorious inheritance in his holy people." Ephesians 1:18

- "Do not lose the courage you had in the past, which has a great reward." Hebrews 10:35 NCV

- "Make this your common practice: Confess your sins to each other and pray for each other so that you can live together whole and healed. The prayer of a person living right with God is something powerful to be reckoned with." James 5:16–18 MSG

- "'For I know the plans I have for you,' declares the Lord, 'plans to prosper you and not to harm you, plans to give you hope and a future. Then you will call on me and come and pray to me, and I will listen to you.'" Jeremiah 29:11–12

- "No one has ever seen God; but if we love one another, God lives in us and his love is made complete in us." 1 John 4:12

## ON FAITH

- "Though one may be overpowered, two can defend themselves. A cord of three strands is not quickly broken." Ecclesiastes 4:12

- "Now faith is confidence in what we hope for and assurance about what we do not see." Hebrews 11:1

- "He has shown you, O mortal, what is good. And what does the Lord require of you? To act justly and to love mercy and to walk humbly with your God." Micah 6:8

- "For it is God who works in you to will and to act in order to fulfill his good purpose." Philippians 2:13

- "Plans fail for lack of counsel, but with many advisers they succeed." Proverbs 15:22

- "In their hearts humans plan their course, but the Lord establishes their steps." Proverbs 16:9

- "Many are the plans in a person's heart, but it is the Lord's purpose that prevails." Proverbs 19:21

- "Where there is no revelation, people cast off restraint; but blessed is the one who heeds wisdom's instruction." Proverbs 29:18

- "Let the morning bring me word of your unfailing love, for I have put my trust in you. Show me the way I should go, for to you I entrust my life. Rescue me from my enemies, Lord, for I hide myself in you. Teach me to do your will, for you are my God; may your good Spirit lead me on level ground. For your name's sake, Lord, preserve my life; in your righteousness, bring me out of trouble. In your unfailing love, silence my enemies; destroy all my foes, for I am your servant." Psalm 143:8–12

## ON FEAR AND EVIL

- "The weapons we fight with are not the weapons of the world. On the contrary, they have divine power to demolish strongholds. We demolish arguments and every pretension that sets itself up against the knowledge of God, and we take captive every thought to make it obedient to Christ." 2 Corinthians 10:4–5

- "Be strong and courageous. Do not be afraid or terrified because of them, for the Lord your God goes with you; he will never leave you nor forsake you. . . . The Lord himself goes before you and will be with you; he will never leave you nor forsake you. Do not be afraid; do not be discouraged." Deuteronomy 31:6, 8

- "Moses said, 'Do not follow the crowd in doing wrong.'" Exodus 23:2

- "You intended to harm me, but God intended it for good to accomplish what is now being done, the saving of many lives." Genesis 50:20

- "For we know him who said, 'It is mine to avenge; I will repay.'" Hebrews 10:30

- "Where there is strife, there is pride, but wisdom is found in those who take advice." Proverbs 13:10

- "When the wicked rise to power, people go into hiding; but when the wicked perish, the righteous thrive." Proverbs 28:28

- "Fear of man will prove to be a snare, but whoever trusts in the Lord is kept safe." Proverbs 29:25

- "For by the grace given me I say to every one of you: Do not think of yourself more highly than you ought, but rather think of yourself with sober judgment, in accordance with the faith God has distributed to each of you." Romans 12:3

- "But if you do wrong, be afraid, for rulers do not bear the sword for no reason. They are God's servants, agents of wrath to bring punishment on the wrongdoer." Romans 13:4

## FRUIT OF THE SPIRIT BLESSINGS

- "The fruit of the Spirit is love, joy, peace, forbearance, kindness, goodness, faithfulness, gentleness and self-control. Against such things there is no law." Galatians 5:22–23

- "But the wisdom that comes from heaven is first of all pure; then peace-loving, considerate, submissive, full of mercy and good fruit, impartial and sincere." James 3:17

- "Rejoice in the Lord always. I will say it again: Rejoice! Let your gentleness be evident to all. The Lord is near. Do not be anxious about anything, but in everything, by prayer and petition, with thanksgiving, present your requests to God. And the peace of God, which transcends all understanding, will guard your hearts and your minds in Christ Jesus. Finally, brothers and sisters, whatever is true, whatever is noble, whatever is right, whatever is pure, whatever is lovely, whatever is admirable—if anything is excellent or praiseworthy—think about such things. Whatever you have learned or received or heard from me, or seen in me—put it into practice. And the God of peace will be with you." Philippians 4:4–9

- "Wait for the Lord, and he will make things right." Proverbs 20:22 NCV

- "Enjoy serving the Lord, and he will give you what you want." Psalm 37:4 NCV

- "Your kingdom is built on what is right and fair. Love and truth are in all you do." Psalm 89:14 NCV

## PRAYER OF JABEZ

- "Jabez was more honorable than his brothers. His mother had named him Jabez, saying, 'I gave birth to him in pain.' Jabez cried out to the God of Israel, 'Oh, that you would bless me and enlarge my territory! Let your hand be with me, and keep me from harm so that I will be free from pain.' And God granted his request." 1 Chronicles 4:9–10

## TRUST

- "Trust in the Lord with all your heart, and do not lean on your own understanding. In all your ways acknowledge him, and he will make straight your paths." Proverbs 3:5–6 ESV

- "Commit your way to the Lord; trust in him, and he will act." Psalm 37:5 ESV

- "For to set the mind on the flesh is death, but to set the mind on the Spirit is life and peace." Romans 8:6 ESV

## WISDOM—JAMES 3:13–18

**Two Kinds of Wisdom: NIV translation**

"Who is wise and understanding among you? Let them show it by their good life, by deeds done in the humility that comes from wisdom. But if you harbor bitter envy and selfish ambition in your hearts, do not boast about it or deny the truth. Such 'wisdom' does not come down from heaven but is earthly, unspiritual, demonic. For where you have envy and selfish ambition, there you find disorder and every evil practice.

But the wisdom that comes from heaven is first of all pure; then peace-loving, considerate, submissive, full of mercy and good fruit, impartial and sincere. Peacemakers who sow in peace reap a harvest of righteousness."

**Live Well, Live Wisely: MSG translation**

"Do you want to be counted wise, to build a reputation for wisdom? Here's what you do: Live well, live wisely, live humbly. It's the way you live, not the way you talk, that counts. Mean-spirited ambition isn't wisdom. Boasting that you are wise isn't wisdom. Twisting the truth to make yourselves sound wise isn't wisdom. It's the furthest thing from wisdom—it's animal cunning, devilish plotting. Whenever you're trying to look better than others or get the better of others, things fall apart, and everyone ends up at the others' throats.

Real wisdom, God's wisdom, begins with a holy life and is characterized by getting along with others. It is gentle and reasonable, overflowing with mercy and blessings, not hot one day and cold the next, not two-faced. You can develop a healthy, robust community that lives right with God and enjoy its results only if you do the hard work of getting along with each other, treating each other with dignity and honor."

## IN OTHERS' WORDS

## BASICS OF BELIEF

- God is Love.

- Christ dwells in me and delights in me.

- Grace is God's action in my life.

- Hope is certainty in a good future.

- We live in the strong unshakeable Kingdom of God.

- Ruthlessly eliminate hurry from your life. Create space for God.

- To stay in God's presence, sleep, slow down, create solitude, and unplug.

- We bump into reality when we are wrong. —Dallas Willard

- Spiritual disciplines are soul-training exercises. —Dallas Willard

- To repent is to change your mind.

- The Way is the presence, power, and provision of God.

- Kingdom economics are what we need when we need it.

- To be a community of forgiveness, Christians require unity on essentials, liberty on nonessentials, and in all things, charity. —St. Ambrose

*James Bryan Smith, Apprentice Institute, quoting from many sources*

## SIGNIFICANCE

- "Our first half is about making a living. Our second half has the promise of being about how to make a life." —Bob Buford

- "Not all time in life is equal. How many opportunities do you get to talk about what your life is going to add up to with people asking the same question?" —Jim Collins

- "Many people measure their success by wealth, recognition, power, and status. There's nothing wrong with those, but if that's all you're focused on, you're missing the boat . . . if you focus on significance—using your time and talent to serve others—that's when truly meaningful success can come your way." —Ken Blanchard

- "The human tendency, largely driven by ego, is to believe we can do it all. It may be humbling to admit there are only a few things you do really well, but you free yourself to focus on those things, which will lead to greater personal success and significance." — Bob Buford

## MISSIONARY BILL BORDEN

- "No reserve. No retreat. No regrets."

## BOB BUFORD

- "What's the one thing—not two things, not three, not four, but the one big thing—in the box?"

- "Respect the externals of the natural world and the authority of the supernatural world. Doing so will free you to grow and serve well in the second half."

- "The second half is riskier because it has to do with living beyond the immediate. It is about releasing the seed of creativity and energy implanted within us—watering and cultivating it so that we may be abundantly fruitful. It involves investing our gifts in service to others—and receiving the personal joy that comes as a result of that spending. This is the kind of risk for which entrepreneurs much of the time earn excellent returns."

## EDMUND BURKE

- "All that is necessary for the triumph of evil is that good men do nothing."

- "So much of the history of the struggle between good and evil can be explained by Edmund Burke's observation. Time and again those who profess to be good seem to clearly outnumber those who are evil, yet those who are evil seem to prevail far too often. Seldom is it the numbers that determine the outcome, but whether those who claim to be good men are willing to stand up and fight for what they know to be right. There are numerous examples of this sad and awful scenario being played out over and over again in the scriptures." —Wayne Greeson, pastor and attorney

## GEORGE WASHINGTON CARVER

- "May God ever bless, keep, guide, and continue to prosper you in your uplifting work for humanity, be it great or small, is my daily prayer. And may those whom he has redeemed learn to walk with him not only daily or hourly, but momently through the things he has created."

- "Where there is no vision, there is no hope."

- "It is simply service that measures success."

- "Think it, say it, and do it."

- Eight cardinal virtues to emulate and strive toward:

  1. Be clean both inside and out.
  2. Neither look up to the rich nor down on the poor.
  3. Lose, if need be, without squealing.
  4. Win without bragging.
  5. Always be considerate of women, children, and older people.

6. Be too brave to lie.

7. Be too generous to cheat.

8. Take your share of the world and let others take theirs.

## DR. TONY EVANS

- "Freedom, open to grace, is choosing to do what you ought to do."

## PETER DRUCKER

- "Freedom is not fun. It is not the same as individual happiness, nor is it security or peace or progress . . . It is responsible choice. Freedom is not so much right as a duty. Real freedom is not freedom from something; that would be license. It is freedom to choose between doing or not doing something, to act one way or another, to hold one belief or the opposite. It is never a release and always a responsibility. It is not 'fun,' but the heaviest burden laid on man; to decide his own individual conduct as well as the conduct of society and to be responsible for both decisions. The only basis of freedom is the Christian concept of man's nature: imperfect, weak, a sinner, and dust destined into dust, yet made in God's image and responsible for his actions."

## MARTIN LUTHER KING JR.

- "Faith is taking the first step even when you can't see the whole staircase."

- "To be a Christian without prayer is no more possible than to be alive without breathing."

- "The time is always right to do the right thing."

- "Life's most persistent and urgent question is, 'What are you doing for others?'"

- "No person has the right to rain on your dreams."

- "Forgiveness is not an occasional act; it is a constant attitude."

- "Let no man pull you so low as to hate him."

- "Injustice anywhere is a threat to justice everywhere."

- "In the end, we will remember not the words of our enemies, but the silence of our friends."

- "Love is the only force capable of transforming an enemy into a friend."

## ABRAHAM LINCOLN

- "I believe the will of God prevails; without him all human reliance is vain. Without the assistance of that divine being I cannot succeed. With that existence I cannot fail."

- "The best thing about the future is it comes one day at a time."

## BOB PIERCE

- "Don't fail to do something just because you can't do everything."

## JOHN M. TEMPLETON

- "You are sought after if you reflect love, joy, peace, patience, kindness, goodness, faithfulness, gentleness, and self-control."

## MOTHER TERESA

"People are often unreasonable, irrational, and self-centered.
Forgive them anyway.
If you are kind, people may accuse you of selfish, ulterior motives.
Be kind anyway.
If you are successful, you will win some unfaithful friends and some
genuine enemies. Succeed anyway.
If you are honest and sincere, people may deceive you.
Be honest and sincere anyway.
What you spend years creating, others could destroy overnight.
Create anyway.
If you find serenity and happiness, some may be jealous.
Be happy anyway.
The good you do today will often be forgotten.
Do good anyway.
Give the best you have, and it will never be enough.
Give your best anyway.
In the final analysis, it is between you and God.
It was never between you and them anyway."

- "I pray that you will understand the words of Jesus, 'Love one another as I have loved you.' Ask yourself, 'How has he loved me? Do I really love others in the same way?' Unless this love is among us, we can kill ourselves with work and it will only be work, not love. Work without love is slavery."

## BOOKER T. WASHINGTON

- "If you want to lift yourself up, lift up someone else."

- "I will permit no man to narrow and degrade my soul by making me hate him."

- "The world cares very little about what a man or woman knows; it is what a man or woman is able to do that counts."

- "No man who continues to add something to the material, intellectual, and moral well-being of the place in which he lives is left long without proper reward."

- "No greater injury can be done to any youth than to let him feel that because he belongs to this or that race he will be advanced in life regardless of his own merits or efforts."

## JOHN WESLEY

"I am no longer my own, but thine.
Put me to what thou wilt, rank me with whom thou wilt.
Put me to doing, put me to suffering.
Let me be employed by thee or laid aside by thee.
Exalted for thee or brought low for thee.

Let me be full, let me be empty.

Let me have all things, let me have nothing.

I freely and heartily yield all things to thy pleasure and disposal.

And now, O glorious and blessed God,

Father, Son, and Holy Spirit,

Thou art mine, and I am thine.

So be it.

And the covenant which I have made on earth,

Let it be ratified in heaven. Amen."

—A Covenant Prayer

- "Do all the good you can, by all the means you can, in all the ways you can, in all the places you can, at all the times you can, to all the people you can, as long as ever you can."

- "Earn all you can, give all you can, save all you can."

- "Get all you can without hurting your soul, your body, or your neighbor. Save all you can, cutting off every needless expense. Give all you can. Be glad to give, and ready to distribute; laying up in store for yourselves a good foundation against the time to come, that you may attain eternal life."

- "I have so much to do that I spend several hours in prayer before I am able to do it."

- "I judge all things only by the price they shall gain in eternity."

- "Let your words be the genuine picture of your heart."

- "On every occasion of uneasiness, we should retire to prayer, that we may give place to the grace and light of God and then form our resolutions, without being in any pain about what success they may have. In the greatest temptations, a single look to Christ, and the barely pronouncing his name, suffices to overcome the wicked one, so it be done with confidence and calmness of spirit."

- "It cannot be that the people should grow in grace unless they give themselves to reading. A reading people will always be a knowing people."

- "Beware you be not swallowed up in books! An ounce of love is worth a pound of knowledge."

- "What one generation tolerates the next generation will embrace."

# ACKNOWLEDGMENTS

No life takes shape in a vacuum; certainly no book does, particularly a book about making life matter. To the people in these pages, seen and unseen, *Plan of Action* is one more effect of your lives and influence. Thank you. Your names on these pages show category, not rank. Some names should appear multiple times; others may be MIA because unlike gratitude, space has limits.

Foremost thanks to my wife, Debbie, and to our children, Grace and Jake, for truth with love and understanding in the drafting of this book. Across the family, special thanks to Mom, to my brother, Stan, and to my sisters, Nancie and Sandra. Thanks to my brothers-in-law, Dan, Mike, Jim, and David, and to my sisters-in-law, Jill, Tara, and Shelley. Across the nation, a shout-out to aunts, uncles, cousins, nieces, nephews, and all new arrivals. You're in and out of our lives and stay close to our hearts.

Of course, I'm blessed for the great partnership, skill, and talent of writer Nancy Lovell, enlivening *Plan of Action* with ideas, research, and drawing out great stories, and for my custom-fit editorial board, professionals willing to weigh in as the sausage got made: Debbie Dellinger, Clayton Smith, Rhonda Kehlbeck, Steve Cole, Allison Rickels, and Brad Clark.

Thank you to the friends and neighbors we do life with: the Blakeman-Hunters, Clarks, Dunnings, Fosters, Kirbys, Kramers, Laufers, Mahers, McDonnells, Ringer-Suarezes, Smiths, Vander Arks, Vialles, Illardis, Luebberings, Seferovichs, Shafrans, and Unruhs.

Further into Kansas City, I'm grateful for partnerships with the likes of Adam Hamilton, Jeff Kirby, Debbi Nixon, Chris Folmsbee, Brad Bergman, Steve Eiginoire, and Doug Smith; Frank Brown, Brian Hague, and Ray Reuter; David Wooddell and Chuck Connealy; Todd Zylstra, Carol Walker, Brent Vander Ark, and Allan Chugg; Alan Barkema; Bob Petersen; Mike Fox and Spencer Kerley; Tom Nelson; Sarah Rowland, and Missy Hughes Smith.

Thank you to the many professionals in our life circle: Chad Burt, Jessica Hejna, Ryan Meda, Brad Bergman, Tom Lipscomb, John Goodwin, and Jeff Imlay; Drs. Glenn Goldstein, Jeffrey Graves, Shawn Sabin, Ross Headley, Mike Monaco, Johann Ohly, and Bradley Seaman; Colette Majerle, Ann Tillery, and Mindy Yowell; Lyle Pishny, Joseph Growney, and Justin Whitney; and Todd Ruskamp.

In philanthropy, where we can add to the common good and human flourishing, thank you to Christian Wiggins, Bob Off, Chad Harris, Greg Bamford, Ryan Downs, Michael Dykes, Mike Fayhee, Don Ferguson, Jim Herbert, Dick Kruse, Robert Lewis, Rod Penner, and Doug Sims; Stan Wallace, Liam Atchison, and Keith Campbell; Debbie Dellinger and Mark Linsz; Paul Forbes, Matt Farmer, and Greg James; Jay Bennett, Margie Blanchard, Dean Niewolny, Dale Dawson, John Leffin, Loyd Reeb, and Jeff Spadafora; David Smith; Carol Hallett; and Keith Chancey.

For talent in the marketplace, the arena to activate higher standards of living to drive freedom and liberty, I'm grateful to triple-impact business leaders such as Drew Hiss, Dan Cooper, Tim James, and Jenny Trupka. And to Joe Calhoon; Aimee Minnich and Bill High; Henry Kaestner and Luke Roush; Brad Clark, Craig Clark, and Cole Hawks; Kevin Rauckman and Rod Brenneman.

Finally, warm gratitude to the many great colleagues for a season and reason: Ken Hersch, Bob Edwards, Mark Zenuk, and Cameron Dunn; Alan Boyce; Craig Huss; Kim Kuebler; Randy Marten and Jeff Muchow; Eric Bowles and Martha Carpenter Smith; Dusty Clevenger, Luanne Eskew, John Shealy, Michael Preisinger, Larry Tubbs, and Don Wille; Chris Erickson; and Ejnar Knutson.

Thanks to Steve Bresky; Richard Brock; Greg Heckman; Phil Lindau; Greg Mellinger; Bruce Scherr; Steve Campbell and Ed Kurtz; Mayo Schmidt and Fran Malecha; Mike Walters; Steve Bobb, Kevin Kaufman, John Miller, and Matt Rose; Tom Caron, Drew Collier, Diane Knutson, and Brian McDonald; Mark Drabenstott; and Steve Moore.

Thanks to Bob Ludington, Todd McQueen, Frank Heindel, Eric Jackson, John Messerich, Steve Dunn, Randy Spiegel, Monte Wetter, Jim Harding, George Schieber, Ron Bingham, Bart Brummer, Mark Mossman, Wyatt Brummer, Julie Heiliger, Jen Gutekunst, Brian Smith, Greg Lickteig, Eric Perry, Kevin Thompson, and Charlie Osborne; Duane Fischer, John Heck, Joan Maclin, Tim Regan, Roger Barber, Randy Foster, Tom DiGiorgio, Theresa Ruby, and Mickey Ebenkamp; Marshall Faith, David Faith, Laura Alley, Neal Harlan, Jim Chastain, Chuck Elsea, and Jack Zenner; Brian Aust, Todd Becker, Bill Krueger, Paul Schlee, Mike Meyers, Steve Dupnick, Tom Gugger, Jim Shanley, and Don Soukup.

Thanks to Jack Bienkowski, Jeff Borchardt, Mike Braude, Dan Brophy, Charles Carey, Christine Cochran, De'Ana Dow, Tom Erickson, Kent Horsager, Jula Kinnaird, Dave Lyons, John Miller, Tom Neal, and Jim Newsome; and Paul DeBruce and Bill Winnie.

Thanks to Russ Bragg, Don Brummer, Jim Blackwell, Roy Cook, Jim Warner, Jim Anderson, Ned Skinner, Gary Redman, Jerry Osborne, and Red Geurts; Bill Dewey, Pete Gagliano, Helen Pound, Jay O'Neil, and Doug Upena; Nic Folland, Don Wenneker, Doug Cole, Bill Criscione, Tim Briggs, and Bill Kessel.

Thanks to Bob Pagan, Greg Muench, Al Ambrose, Allen Anderson, Russ Henshaw, Mike Long, Mark Huston, Allen Hurley, Brenda Grubbs, Lynn Howard, Rick Shoemaker, and Bill Lyons.

Every chapter in this book, on the lines and between them, shows the often intangible and astonishing effects of community. If your name is in the list, believe me, you're on every page. List or no, if you're in my life, you're in this book.

## RANDY LINVILLE

Randy Linville, former farm kid, is a trader, corporate head, and nonprofit and community champion of every size team and dream. As CEO of Scoular, he diversified and steadied the ag supply chain company into US and international markets. As founding chair of the Commodity Markets Council, he united industry rivals to compete in the world market. After his career, he helped form and sell one of the first private equity–backed consolidators taking agribusiness to world markets. He served on nonprofit boards such as The FarmHouse Foundation, Global Scholars, the Halftime Institute, and the World Soy Foundation. His current role is managing director of ClearSight Ventures. Randy is a husband, father, traveler, and collector of insights.

Connect with Randy at: **www.linkedin.com/in/randallinville.**

## NANCY LOVELL

Nancy Lovell is a writer, media professional, best-selling ghostwriter, and editor whose clients' works have appeared in The *New York Times*, *The Washington Post*, and *The Dallas Morning News*.

As cofounder of the nationally recognized Lovell-Fairchild Communications, she wrote and placed op-eds in *USA Today* and *The*

*Wall Street Journal*, provided media training, and advised in successful launch campaigns involving figures such as Robert Duvall, Patricia Heaton, T.D. Jakes, Jim Caviezel, and Dr. Oz. Her firm's film clients included Universal Studios, Sony Pictures, and Samuel Goldwyn.

Nancy was a lead writer and communications advisor for Bob Buford's Halftime organization, and she has served numerous entertainment, technical, and corporate clients. She holds a degree in advertising and public relations from Texas Tech University. Having grown up in Japan, Texas, and Illinois, she now calls Dallas home. *Plan of Action* is her third book.